My J<

Born on 15 October 1931, at Rameswaram in Tamil Nadu, **Dr Avul Pakir Jainulabdeen Abdul Kalam** specialized in aeronautical engineering from Madras Institute of Technology. Dr Kalam is one of the most distinguished scientists of India and has received honorary doctorates from forty-five universities and institutions in India and abroad. He has been awarded the Padma Bhushan (1981), the Padma Vibhushan (1990) and India's highest civilian award, the Bharat Ratna (1997). He has also received the King Charles II medal (2007), the Woodrow Wilson Award (2008), the Hoover Award (2008) and the International Von Karman Wings Award (2009) among other international accolades.

Dr Kalam became the eleventh President of India on 25 July 2002. His focus and greatest ambition remains finding ways to transform India into a developed nation.

My Journey

Transforming Dreams into Actions

A.P.J. Abdul Kalam

Illustrated by
Priya Sebastian

RUPA

Published by
Rupa Publications India Pvt. Ltd 2013
7/16, Ansari Road, Daryaganj
New Delhi 110002

Sales Centres:

Allahabad Bengaluru Chennai
Hyderabad Jaipur Kathmandu
Kolkata Mumbai

Text copyright © A.P.J. Abdul Kalam 2013
Illustrations copyright © Rupa Publications India Pvt. Ltd 2013

All rights reserved.
No part of this publication may be reproduced, transmitted,
or stored in a retrieval system, in any form or by any means,
electronic, mechanical, photocopying, recording or otherwise,
without the prior permission of the publisher.

ISBN: 978-81-291-2491-3

Third impression 2014

10 9 8 7 6 5 4 3

The moral right of the author has been asserted.

Printed at Thomson Press India Ltd

This book is sold subject to the condition that it shall not, by way
of trade or otherwise, be lent, resold, hired out, or otherwise circulated,
without the publisher's prior consent, in any form of binding or cover
other than that in which it is published.

To the sixteen million youth who I have met and
interacted with in the last two decades

contents

introduction

My Journey recounts certain unique experiences of my life from my childhood until now, when I am over eighty years old. In all these years and through all these experiences, the most important lesson I have learnt is, one must keep dreaming at various phases of life, and then work hard to realize those dreams. If we do so, then success is imminent. To the many people I meet I always say, 'Dreams are not those that we see in our sleep; they should be the ones that never let us sleep.'

The idea for this book came to me one day while I was walking in my garden. Like every other time, I stood under the grand Arjuna tree which is nearly a hundred years old in age, and I looked up into its branches to see if any new nests had been built by birds or if a fresh beehive had appeared. And something in that moment, as I gazed up at this tree, in this city of Delhi, reminded me intensely of my father. He, too, was an early riser whose first few hours of the day would be spent with nature, examining his coconut trees, walking the roads of the town we lived in. I recalled with a smile and a feeling of happiness my childhood, the people who inhabited it, the hands I held while I traversed it. I then also began to think of the journey that my life has been—the unusual paths I have travelled, the things I have seen, the events I have been a part of. And I began to wonder if these memories and experiences should stay with me or if I must share them with my numerous readers and family members whose numbers have grown as large as the abundant roots of an enormous banyan tree—its great-great-grandchildren!

I have written a few books till date, and in some of them I have described my childhood experiences. When I wrote my first book about my life, I had wondered how it would interest anyone. Unlike in my previous books, *My Journey* focuses more on the smaller, lesser-known happenings in my life. The incidents around my mother and father were written because even now, at the age of eighty-two, I still cherish the values and ethics that they lovingly inculcated in me. The qualities they instilled in me, and which I learnt from observing them and by understanding their reactions to the adversities they faced, have helped me live better, and through these values my parents still live strongly within me. When my father talked about the importance of understanding people's minds, or faced difficulties stoically, I remembered his words years later when I was battling various odds myself. In my mother's tender touch and sensitive upbringing of her children I found a world of love and kindness. I also felt compelled to record in detail the contributions of my sister Zohra and her generosity; the openness of the outlook of my first mentor Ahmed Jalalluddin that first encouraged me to think of studying further. Instances such as my failure to qualify for the Indian Air Force and the other adversities I have been witness to, have all brought home to me the necessity of setbacks in one's life. Yes, they seem insurmountable at the time, but there really is no difficulty one cannot overcome if there is determination in the heart.

Recently, I was talking to my friend Professor Arun Tiwari, when he suddenly asked me an unusual question, 'Kalam saheb, can you sum up your life so far, in one sentence?'

It made me think for a while. Eventually I said, 'Arun, my life can be summed up in these phrases and words: love poured to the child…struggle…more struggle…bitter tears… then sweet tears…and finally a life as beautiful and fulfilling as seeing the birth of the full moon.'

I hope these stories will help all my readers understand

their dreams and compel them to work on those dreams that keep them awake.

A.P.J. Abdul Kalam

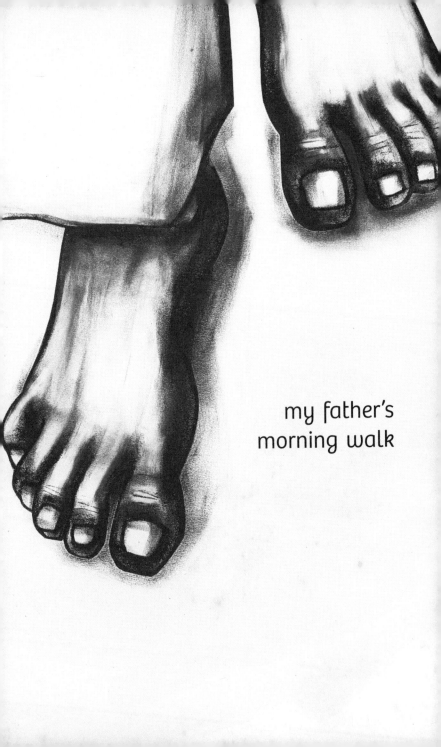

my father's
morning walk

For as far back as I can remember, my father Jainulabdeen's day began at 4 a.m. He would be up before anyone else in the household. After saying his prayers in the breaking light of the day, he would go on a long walk to visit his coconut grove. We lived in Rameswaram, a small temple town on an island in Tamil Nadu. This being on the east coast of India, dawn would break early, and our day's schedule followed the rhythm of the rising and setting of the sun and the sea waves.

The sound of the sea was a constant presence in our lives. Storms and cyclones blew by with regularity during the tumultuous monsoon months. We lived in our ancestral home, a fairly large house made of limestone and brick, built some time in the nineteenth century. It was never luxurious, but was filled with love. My father had a boat-building business. Additionally, we also owned a small coconut grove some four miles away from our house. That was where my father would be headed for in the early morning hours. His walking circuit was well established and he rarely deviated from it. First he would step out into Mosque Street, where our house was located. It was a small, predominantly Muslim locality not too far from the Shiva temple that has made our town famous for centuries. He would then walk through the narrow lanes of the town, on to the more open roads leading to the coconut groves, and finally wind his way through the groves to his patch of land.

Today I try to imagine him walking on those quiet roads, long before the day made its many demands on him. Ours was a large family and I am sure there were many pressures on him to see to our needs. But at that hour, I think of him listening intently to the sea, to the ever-present ravens and other birds that swooped and flew all around, woken up by the rising sun like him. Perhaps he said his prayers to himself as he walked, or thought of his family with a calm, uncluttered early morning mind. I never did ask him what went through his mind on this long daily walk—for when does a young boy really have the time to reflect in this way about his father? But I was always sure that the morning walk added something to his personality, an element of calm that was apparent even to strangers.

My father was not a person with much formal education; neither did he ever acquire much wealth in his long lifetime. Yet, he was one of the wisest, truly generous men I have had the fortune of knowing. Our mosque was the focal point of the locality, and my father was the man everyone turned to in their hour of need. They believed that he was truly connected to God. I remember going to the mosque to say my prayers with him. He made sure we never missed any of our prayers and neither did it enter our minds to shirk this duty. After saying our namaz, when we would step out on to the road, groups of people would inevitably be there, waiting to talk to him and share their worries with him.

What did these men and women see in him? He was not a preacher, nor a teacher. He was just a man who lived by his convictions and the tenets of his religion. What did he give them? I now think that it was his mere presence that calmed them and gave them hope. He said prayers for them, and many people would offer him bowls of water. He would dip his fingertips in them and say a prayer, after which the water would be taken away to be given to the sick. Later, many of these people would come to the house and thank him for having cured their near and dear ones.

Why did he do this? And where did he get the peacefulness and generosity of heart to talk to people, comfort them and pray for them, in the midst of the busyness of his own life? He was a humble boat owner. Life was certainly not easy for him, what with finding the best ways to make ends meet in a tiny temple town cut off from the mainland. Yet, never once did I see my father turn away anyone who wanted to unburden himself by talking to him.

Without doubt, he was a deeply spiritual man with some kind of connection with God. I believe his spirituality came from being a learned man. He knew the scriptures and could bring out their essential truth to even the youngest enquiring mind. When I asked him questions, he would always reply and attempt to explain in simple, straightforward Tamil. Once I asked him, 'Why do these people come to you? And what do you really do for them?' His reply still stays with me, nearly five decades later.

'Whenever human beings find themselves alone, as a natural reaction, they start looking for company. Whenever they are in trouble, they look for someone to help them... Every recurrent anguish, longing and desire finds it own special helper. For the people who come to me in distress, I am but a go-between in their effort to ward off demonic forces with prayers and offerings.'

Then he went on to tell me something about prayers and its power over man that still resonates, despite my years in the field of scientific research. He said to look for help outside is never the final answer. 'One must understand the difference between a fear-ridden vision of destiny and the vision that enables us to seek the enemy of fulfillment within ourselves... When troubles come, try to understand the relevance of your sufferings. Adversity always presents opportunities for introspection.'

His advice meant that in the many setbacks and defeats that destiny has handed me, I have always been able to look within for strength. I travelled far, far away from life in Rameswaram. My journey took me to places I had never imagined visiting—from the cockpit of a fighter jet to the highest office in the nation. Yet, it was always his words that came back to me.

'There is a divine power that looks over us, that gently lifts us from our sadness and failures and miseries. If we open our minds and let it, it will guide us to our true place. Release yourself from the bindings that limit you and let that power overtake your mind, and that's when you will be on the road to true happiness and peace.' This is what I imagine him saying to me whenever I am worried.

I am now eighty-two years of age. Like him, my day, even today, begins with a walk. Every morning I savour the sight of the new sun, the benign light in the sky before the sun appears, the cool breeze and the sweet call of the birds. I understand how this short time of the day binds us to nature. Each morning is different in the way the elements come together for that day. It is a little drama nature puts up only for us, and I can't stop marvelling at it. Unlike him, I often find myself in different cities and towns in the mornings because of my travels, but the early morning peace and calm is the same everywhere. Wherever I am, I can find a tree that is great with age, where birds dwell and go busily about their day with the new dawn, whose leaves wave gently to me in the morning breeze. It may be a warm day or a bitterly cold misty morning when my breath fogs the air in front of me, but this time away from the cares and worries that the rest of the day will invariably bring means so much to me.

At my home in Delhi there is a grand old Arjuna tree. Somehow my feet always pull me towards it when I walk in my garden. It is usually laden with honeycombs and is home to hundreds of birds, especially parrots. The dignity, beauty and stature of this tree brings memories of my father to mind and I even have silent conversations with it. Once, I wrote this poem, where I imagined what the tree would say to me if only it could:

Oh my friend Kalam,
I crossed age hundred like your father and mother.
Every day morning, you walk an hour,
I also see you on full moon nights,
Walking with a thinking mood.

I know, my friend, the thoughts in your mind,
'What can I give?'...

(The Great Tree in My Home)

As I walk wherever my life has led me, I often think of my father Jainulabdeen. In my mind's eye I see a simple man, who, even when he was of a great age, continued to walk every morning to his coconut grove. As I see him, I imagine how it's been almost an hour since he set off, and the caretaker of the grove is also up and going about his day. When my father walks into his plantation, the men hail each other with warmth. Perhaps Jainulabdeen sits down somewhere awhile. The other man climbs a coconut tree. He chooses half a dozen coconuts and cuts them down with a swing of his knife. They fall with a thump to the ground. The man quickly makes his way down. Then he proceeds to tie them up together into a neat bundle. Now the two men sit companionably for a while. They discuss the state of the trees. They peer up at the sky, talk about rains and pests and other matters of the soil. Finally Jainulabdeen picks up his bundle of coconuts, says goodbye and begins his walk back home. He will give away a few coconuts to neighbours and others. The rest will find their way into curries and chutneys prepared by my mother. I still remember sitting down to those simple meals and enjoying immensely the smooth, creamy coconut chutney my mother placed on the leaf plate. It is a taste that has lingered in my mouth even years later, made sweeter still knowing that it contained the love of my parents and their honest hard work.

the boat

Living on the island of Rameswaram while I was growing up, the sea was an important part of our lives. Its tides, the lapping of the waves, the sound of trains passing on the Pamban Bridge, the birds that always circled the town and the salt in the air are sights and sounds that will always remain linked with my memories of childhood. Apart from its sheer presence around us, the sea was also a source of livelihood for our neighbours and us. Almost every household had some connection with the sea, whether as fishermen or as boat owners.

My father, too, operated a ferry that took people back and forth between the islands of Rameswaram and Dhanushkodi, which is about twenty-two kilometres away. I still remember the time when he got the idea for this, and how we built that boat.

Rameswaram has, since antiquity, been an important pilgrimage destination. Rama is believed to have stopped here and built the bridge to Lanka when he was on his way to rescue Sita. The temple of Rameswaram is dedicated to Shiva, and houses a lingam fashioned by Sita herself. Some versions of the Ramayana say that Rama, Lakshmana and Sita stopped here to pray to Shiva on their way back to Ayodhya from Lanka.

People visiting our town would go to Dhanushkodi as part of their pilgrimage. A bath at Sagara-Sangam here is considered sacred. The sangam is the meeting place of the Bay of Bengal and the Indian Ocean. Dhanushkodi is now connected by road and vans take pilgrims there, but way back when I was a child, a ferry was also a good way of reaching the island.

My father, looking to supplement his not very substantial income, decided to start a ferry business. He started building the boat that we needed for this himself, on the seashore.

Watching the boat come to life from pieces of wood and metal was perhaps my first introduction to the world of engineering. Wood was procured and Ahmed Jalalluddin, a cousin, arrived to help my father out. Every day, I would wait impatiently till I could go to the place where the boat was taking shape. Long pieces of wood were cut into the required shape, dried, smoothened and then joined together. Wood fires seasoned the wood that made up the hull and the bulkheads. Slowly the bottom, then the sides and the hull began to form in front of our eyes. Many years later, in my work, I would learn how to make rockets and missiles. Complex mathematics and scientific research would be the bedrock of those engineering marvels. But that boat coming up on a seashore, which would take pilgrims and fishermen back and forth...who is to say it was not as important or momentous in our lives then?

The building of the boat was an important influence for me in another way. It brought Ahmed Jalalluddin into my life. He was much older than me, yet we struck up a friendship. He recognized the inherent desire within me to learn and question, and was always there to lend a patient ear and give words of advice. He could read and write English, and spoke to me about scientists and inventions, literature and medicine. Walking with him in the streets of Rameswaram, or by the seaside, or by our boat as it took shape, my mind began to form ideas and ambitions.

The boat business was a great success. My father employed some men to operate it, and groups of pilgrims would use the service to reach Dhanushkodi. There were days when I would slip in among the crowd and sit with the crew as they steered the boat to and from Rameswaram. I heard the story of Rama and how he built the bridge to Lanka with the help of his army of monkeys; how he brought back Sita and stopped at Rameswaram again, so that they could perform penance for having killed Ravana; how Hanuman was told to bring back a large lingam from far up north, but when he took too long, Sita would not wait and fashioned a lingam with her own hands to worship Shiva. These stories and many others washed around me in different tongues and shapes, as people from all over India used our ferry service. A little boy among so many was always welcome and there would be someone or the other willing to talk to me, share the story of his life and his reasons for making the pilgrimage.

And so the years went by. My school, teachers, Ahmed Jalalluddin and others taught me so many things. But the boat and the people who sailed in it were no less important. In this way, among the waves and the sands, laughter and stories, the days flew by. Then one day, disaster struck.

The Bay of Bengal is hit frequently by cyclones. The months of November and May in particular are dangerous in this regard. I still remember the night of that terrible cyclone vividly. The wind had picked up speed for days, till it became a howling gale. It screamed and whistled in our ears and pulled and hacked at the trees or anything that stood in its way. Soon torrential rain started. We had retreated into our houses much earlier. There was no electricity in those days, and the lamps barely managed to stay alive. In that flickering darkness, with the wind working itself into a frenzy, the sound of the rain lashing down outside, we huddled together and waited for the night to pass. My thoughts travelled again and again to the open seas. Was anyone trapped there? What was it like to be in a storm such as this without your mother's comforting presence close by?

The next morning, after the storm died down, we saw the unbelievable destruction that had been wrought all around us. Trees, houses, plantations were uprooted and devastated. The roads had disappeared under water and debris flown in by winds that had come in at speeds of over 100 miles an hour. But the worst news of all was the one that hit us like a punch to the stomach. Our boat had been washed away. Now when I think of that day, I realize that perhaps my father had known this would happen the night before, while we waited for the storm to pass. In his life he had already witnessed so many storms and cyclones. This was just one of them. Yet, he had tried to calm us children down and had made sure we went to sleep without infecting us with his worries. In the light of the morning, seeing his drawn face and the worries lining his eyes, I tried to gather my thoughts. In my mind I mourned our lost ferry boat fiercely. It felt as though something I had made with my own hands had been gathered up and tossed away thoughtlessly.

Yet, my father's stoicism is what saw us through this crisis too. In time another boat came, and business resumed. Pilgrims and tourists returned. The temple and the mosque filled with worshippers and the markets bustled with men and women, buying and selling once more.

Cyclones and storms struck us again and again. I even learnt to sleep through them. Many years later, in 1964, when I was no longer living in Rameswaram, a massive cyclone struck. This time, it carried away a part of the landmass of Dhanushkodi. A train that was on Pamban Bridge at the time was washed away, with many pilgrims inside. It altered the geography of the area, and Dhanushkodi became a ghost town, never really recovering its former character. Even today, remnants of buildings stand there as monuments to the 1964 cyclone.

My father lost his ferry boat once more in that storm. He had to rebuild his business yet again. I could not do much to help him practically, for I was far removed from that world. But when I struggled to give shape to the Satellite Launch Vehicle (SLV) rocket, or the Prithvi and Agni missiles, when countdowns and take-offs were disrupted, and our rocket launch sites situated by the Arabian Sea and Bay of Bengal in Thumba and Chandipur were rained upon, I always remembered the look on my father's face the day after the storm. It was an acknowledgement of the power of nature, of knowing what it means to live by the sea and make your living from it. Of knowing that there is a larger energy and force that can crush our ambitions and plans in the blink of an eye, and that the only way to survive is to face your troubles and rebuild your life.

a working boy at eight

Every morning a large pile of newspapers, both in English and Tamil, is delivered to me. During my travels abroad I like to stay in touch with news from India, which I do by going online to read news articles and editorials in different magazines and papers. The wealth of information now available at the click of a finger amazes me. As a person closely involved with engineering and science, the march of technology should not surprise me, but when I juxtapose our lives today with what it was like seventy years ago, in a small south Indian town, the difference is startling even for me.

I was born in the year 1931. When I was about eight, World War II broke out. Britain declared war on Nazi Germany, and despite the Indian Congress's opposition, India too, as a British colony, was involved in the war. India's war effort saw a record number of Indian soldiers being deployed in various warzones around the world. Daily life, however, remained fairly unaffected initially, particularly for us in the southern tip of the country.

As I have mentioned, Rameswaram in the 1940s was a sleepy little town that came alive with the arrival of pilgrims. The inhabitants were mostly tradespeople or small businessmen. The town was dominated by the temple, though there was a mosque and a church too. The inhabitants went about their way fairly peacefully, and other than the normal altercations that break out in any town or village, nothing much of importance happened.

The only source of information about the outside world was the newspaper. The agency that distributed newspapers was run by my cousin Samsuddin. Along with Jalalluddin, he was a big influence in my early life. Though he could read and write, Samsuddin was not well travelled nor highly educated. Yet he had such affection for me and encouraged me in so many ways, that he became a guiding light for me. These men understood my deepest thoughts and feelings before I could articulate them. To me they were adults who could reach out beyond the narrow confines of their daily lives and businesses and see the larger world.

Samsuddin's newspaper distribution agency was the only one in Rameswaram. There were about a thousand literate people in the town, and he delivered newspapers to all of them. The papers carried news about the Independence Movement that was heading towards a crescendo at the time. These news items would be read and discussed with great gusto among everyone. There would also be news from the war front, about Hitler and the Nazi army. Of course, there were many mundane matters too, like astrological references or bullion rates, which were consulted with utmost interest. The Tamil paper *Dinamani* was the most popular of all these papers.

The way the papers reached Rameswaram was quite unique. They came by morning train and were kept at Rameswaram station. From there they had to be collected and sent to all the subscribers. This was Samsuddin's business and he managed it effortlessly. However, as World War II raged, we no longer remained isolated from the world, and it affected my life and the newspaper delivery business in a strange new way.

The British government had placed a number of sanctions and rations on goods. Something like a state of emergency now prevailed in the country. Our large family felt the difficulties acutely. Food, clothes, the needs of the babies of the household, all became difficult to procure and provide for. In our family there were five sons and daughters, as well as my father's brothers' families. My grandmother and mother had to stretch every resource to the utmost to keep everyone fed, clothed and in good health.

As the difficulties of the war started affecting us, Samsuddin came up with a proposal that excited and delighted me tremendously. One fallout of the conditions was that the rail stop at Rameswaram station had been done away with. What would happen to our papers then? How were they to be collected and then distributed to all the people of the town who were looking forward to their daily dose of news? Samsuddin found a way out. The papers would be kept ready in large bundles. As the train chugged down the Rameswaram–Dhanushkodi track, they would be flung out on to the platform. And that is where I came in. Samsuddin offered me the enjoyable job of catching these bundles of papers being thrown from the moving train and then taking them around town for distribution!

My enthusiasm knew no bounds. I was only eight, but I was going to contribute in a meaningful way to the household income! For many days I had noticed the amount of food on my mother's and grandmother's plates becoming lesser and lesser as they divided the portions between all of us. The children were always fed first and I don't remember any of us ever going hungry. Obviously, the women were compromising on their nutrition for us. I agreed to Samsuddin's offer with alacrity.

However, my new job had to be fitted into my regular routine. My studies and school had to continue as before, and the delivery business had to be accommodated amidst all these other activities. Among my siblings and cousins, I had shown an early aptitude for mathematics. My father had arranged for me to take tuitions from our mathematics teacher. However, my teacher had a condition that I, along with the four other students whom he had accepted, needed to reach his home at dawn after having taken a bath. So for a year, which the duration of the tuition, I started my day while it was still dark outside, with my mother shaking me awake. She herself would have risen before me and got my bath ready. She would then help me bathe and send me on my way to my teacher's home. There I would study for an hour and return by 5 a.m. By then my father would be ready to take me to the Arabic School nearby, where I learnt the Koran Sharif.

After my lesson on the Koran Sharif was over, I would sprint away to the railway station. There I would wait, hopping from one leg to the other, eyes and ears keenly open for signs of the oncoming train. Surprisingly, unlike most trains these days, the Madras–Dhanushkodi Mail was rarely delayed! Soon, the engine smoke would be visible in the distance. The horn would be tooted loudly and with a thunderous roar, the train would pass through the station. I had worked out the best spot from which to keep an eye out for the flying newspaper bundles. Like clockwork, they would be tossed out on to the platform. The train would then huff and puff away, Samsuddin's person in the train would wave out to me and as the train receded, its whistle growing faint, my job would begin.

I then picked up the bundles, divided them up into batches according to the neighbourhoods in which the papers had to be distributed and off I went. For about an hour I tore around Rameswaram, delivering the papers to everyone. Soon I began to identify people by the papers they read. Many would be waiting for me, and there would be always be a friendly word or two. Some would tell me to hurry back home so I would not be late for school! I think most enjoyed being handed their papers by a cheerful eight year old.

Our town being on the east coast, by the time the work was over at 8 a.m., the sun would be high up in the sky. Now I headed back home, where my mother waited with breakfast. A simple meal would be served, but how hungry I was usually! My mother made sure I ate every morsel before sending me off to school. But my work did not end there.

In the evening, after school was over, I would do the rounds of Samsuddin's customers again, collecting dues. Then I would meet him, so he could work out the accounts of the day.

At that time, sitting somewhere near the sea, with the breeze blowing in, Jalalluddin or Samsuddin would finally open up the day's paper. All of us would pore over the black type of the *Dinamani*. One of them would read aloud the news items, and slowly the larger outside world would enter our consciousness. Gandhi, Congress, Hitler, Periyar E.V. Ramasamy, their words and exhortations would hang in the evening air. I would trace the photos and words with my fingers, wondering what it must be like to be out there in the larger world with all of them. Maybe, I thought to myself, one day I would go to the big cities like Madras, Bombay and Calcutta. What would I say if I ever got to meet people like Gandhi and Nehru? But such thoughts were soon interrupted by the calls of my playmates, and then for dinner. There was homework to be done, and even an eight year old has only that much energy to spend. By 9 p.m. I would be fast asleep, as the next day more studies and the life of a working man lay in store.

This routine continued for about a year. In that one year of running around with the papers, I grew taller and browner. I also learnt that I could now judge quite accurately the distances I could cover at a sprint with a bundle of papers in my hand, and hence could time my arrival at various localities at the same time every day. I could calculate in my head the amount owed to Samsuddin by each of his subscribers, and could reel off the names of those who had not paid up that day. Mostly, I learnt that to be a working man meant you had to be up and ready to face the day, whatever else may happen to you. Homework, tuition, prayers, all carried on, but the Madras–Dhanushkodi Mail would not wait for me—I had to be present at the station at the correct time and at the correct point to catch the bundles as they came flying in. It was my first brush with taking up a responsibility and seeing to it that I kept my word to my cousin Samsuddin, no matter what. It was also a most enjoyable time and I loved every moment of it, notwithstanding the intense tiredness every night. My mother often fretted at my taking up this additional work and the toll it was taking on me, but I shook my head and smiled at her. Knowing that my earnings were somehow helping us all, and that she was secretly proud of me for having taken on the role of a working man at the age of eight, kept me going with a smile on my face.

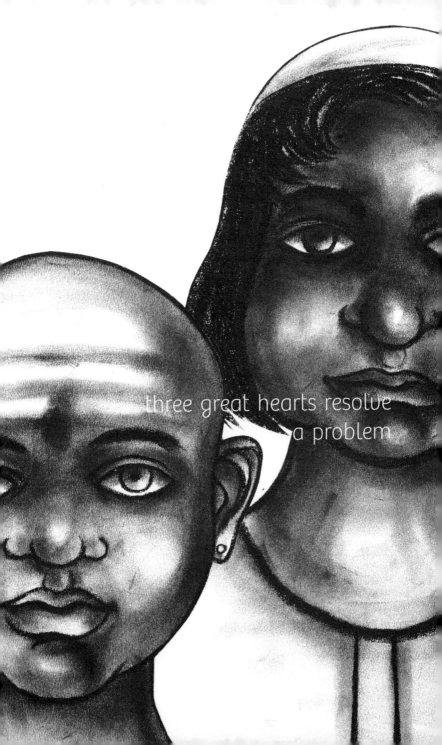

three great hearts resolve
a problem

My childhood town of Rameswaram is a small island. Its highest spot is the top of a hill called Gandamadana Parvatham. Standing there, you could see the whole of Rameswaram stretched out around you—lush green coconut palms swaying everywhere, the sea in the distance and the looming gopuram of the Ramanathaswamy Temple presiding over the skyline. It was a quiet town then. The people made their living from either fishing or coconut farming, and from the tourism that occurred due to the presence of the temple. Rameswaram is one of the holiest pilgrimage spots for many Indians, and the town was almost always full of pilgrims and tourists.

The small local population consisted of mostly Hindu households, with a sprinkling of Muslims like us, and Christians too. Each community lived in healthy contentment next to the other. The divisions and vicissitudes of the outside world rarely made their way here. The daily papers brought news of upheavals and communal fault lines being drawn elsewhere, but here, life continued at its age-old leisurely pace.

This quiet harmony had been in place for generations. My father loved to tell us the story of our great-great-grandfather, who once saved the idol of the Ramanathaswamy Temple. The story went that on a certain festival day, the *vigraha*, or idol, would be taken out of the sanctum sanctorum and carried in a procession around the temple precincts. The temple has a number of tanks dotting it, and the idol was taken around the periphery of these tanks too. During one such procession, in a sequence of events no one remembers clearly any more, the *vigraha* fell into the tank. What a calamity that was! People stood rooted in horror, imagining the wrath of the gods falling upon them very soon. One person, however, did not lose his presence of mind—my great-great-grandfather. He leapt into the tank and retrieved the idol in no time. The gratitude of the priests and other temple officials was overwhelming. Yes, he was a Muslim. And yes, caste and religious purists would be horrified at the most sacred element of the temple being handled by someone not authorized to do so, but none of these feelings were articulated. Instead, my great-great-grandfather was treated like a hero. The temple also made a proclamation that from now on, at the festival, the temple would give *Mudal Marayadai* to him. This was a rare honour for anyone, let alone for someone from a different religion. It meant that on each such festival day, the temple would first honour, or give *marayadai* to my great-great-grandfather. This tradition went on for years and years and the *marayadai* would be given to my father too.

This sense of harmony continued into later years. Like I have mentioned in another chapter, my father had a ferry business in which pilgrims were taken to Dhanushkodi. Our ferry service was used by the temple too.

My father was the imam of the Rameswaram mosque. He was a deeply devout man with complete and utter faith in the Koran. He inculcated all the habits of a good Muslim in his children and indeed in his entire family. For the people of the town, he was a philosopher and guide—someone they could turn to with their problems, whether spiritual or otherwise.

One of his closest friends was the priest of the Ramanathaswamy Temple, Pakshi Lakshmana Sastry. Sastrygal was not only the priest but also a very learned man, well versed in Vedic knowledge. I still remember his visage perfectly. He was always dressed in the traditional attire of a temple priest, in his dhoti and angavastram. On his head he sported the mandatory tuft of the Brahmins, the *kudumi*. He was one of the kindest, most gentle men I knew.

There was a third person who was as important in the spiritual life of our little community and that was Father Bodal, the priest of the lone church in the town. He was as involved in the welfare of the churchgoers of Rameswaram as my father and Sastrygal, and as concerned about the need for harmony and peace in Rameswaram.

The memory of these three learned men is still etched in my mind. I can still see them—one in his turban and imam's cloak, another in his dhoti and the third in his cassock. They met every Friday evening, at around four-thirty, and discussed matters of religion and the happenings of the town. Sometimes people came to visit them at that time with specific issues to be resolved, or the three men kept each other apprised of anything that could potentially threaten the peace among the people and together, they tried to work out ways of clearing miscommunication or scotching rumours before they assumed dangerous proportions. The fundamental requirement for peace—effective communication among sections of the people— was always kept alive by these three patriarchs. Their discussions ranged over a number of topics—the Freedom Movement that was taking the country in an entirely new direction, the attitude of the British government to the calls of the nationalists and how all this affected us, concerned them deeply. They quietly soothed the society around them, making it a harmonious whole where everyone could have an opportunity to speak freely to them.

One incident from my childhood brought this reality close to my life. I was then about eight years old, and studying in the third standard. My best friends were Ramanadha Sastry, Aravindan and Sivaprakasan. All of them were Brahmins, and Ramanadhan, in fact, was Pakshi Lakshmana Sastry's son. We led the usual life of schoolboys, spending most of the day together in the classroom and outside. Like all good friends, our day was incomplete if, at any time, one of us was absent and we could not share with each other the minute details of all that is important for boys of that age. In the classroom, we sat near one another and Ramanadhan and I shared the same bench.

Before I proceed with the main story, I would like to sketch a portrait of my school, which holds such beautiful memories of days of innocence and mischief and learning for me. It was called the Rameswaram Panchayat Primary School and I attended it from 1936 to 1944. It was situated near the seashore, and was not the most sturdy building certainly! Parts of it were built with bricks but the roof was thatched. But it was the only school in Rameswaram in those days and all the children of the town studied there. We were 400 boys and girls in total. Yes, this school had an unimpressive building and scanty amenities but it was an interesting place nonetheless. The teachers, particularly those who taught history, geography and science, were loved by the students. Why? Because they loved teaching and ensured that each one of us excelled in our studies. To give equal attention to the fifty-five children in each class could not have been an easy task. They did not want us to only earn good marks in our exams, they also wanted us to develop a love for the subjects they taught us. We saw the light of purity shining in our teachers.

Even if one student was absent for a day, they would go to the parents and enquire about the child's welfare and the reason for his not coming to school. If one of us got high marks, the teacher would be the first person to go to our homes and share the information with our parents. My school was a happy place. All of us who started our schooling there completed our studies till the eighth standard. I don't remember even a single person dropping out. These days, when I visit schools, both big and small, all across the country, I tell them that true quality does not come from a great building or great facilities or great advertisements. It happens when education is imparted with love by great teachers.

To return to my story, schools of that time, particularly small ones like mine, did not have uniforms. We were free to wear any traditional items required by our religion. My friend Ramanadhan sported a tuft, or *kudumi*, like his father. (Later, when he grew up, he too became the priest of the temple after his father.) I went to school wearing my little woven skullcap, like all Muslim boys of the town. Not once had any of us either noticed or remarked upon this.

When we were in the third standard, there was a great excitement in our lives—we had a new teacher at school. In a small self-contained community, this was a matter of much excitement and discussion. We students were agog with anticipation to know what our new teacher would be like. Would he be strict or lenient? Quick-tempered or patient? We could not wait for him to start teaching us. And the first day he came to the classroom, all our eagerness spilled forth.

The teacher was also a Hindu, a Brahmin. As soon as he entered the classroom, he cast a quick appraising eye over us all, perhaps taking in the diverse attire of this bunch of boys. Today, I think he must have missed noticing the bright eyes and eager smiles of the children—strangely, those are the first things that strike me when confronted by a roomful of children! But our new teacher was quick to get down to business. He walked to the front of the class and the first people his eyes settled on were Ramanadhan and I. We were the star pupils, always eager to learn and participate, and sat right in front. His eyes lingered on my cap and on Ramanadhan's tuft. A look of annoyance, even disbelief, washed over his face. Without giving any reason, he demanded to know my name. When I told him, I was peremptorily told to gather my things and move to the back row, for reasons known only to him.

I felt sad, even humiliated. I wondered why this had happened. Ramanadhan was in tears. I still recall his large eyes awash with tears as I picked up my books and moved away from him.

But neither of us was ready to let this go unreported. That very day I told my father about it, and Ramanadhan told his father too. The men were shocked and dismayed. This went against everything they had worked for! A teacher, who was supposed to be imparting knowledge and opening up our minds, was instead doing just the opposite. We had rarely seen these two mild-mannered gentlemen so agitated. They immediately spoke to one another and confirmed the details of the incident.

The next Friday, when dusk was falling, they met as usual. Father Bodal was present too. The teacher had been summoned, and presented himself. In the gathering darkness, as day turned into night, my father and Sastrygal told him in no uncertain terms that the scourge of religious divisions, which was disturbing India's fabric in other parts of the country, would not be allowed to grow here. They would not allow children to be segregated; they would certainly not tolerate anyone who made religion a divisive factor instead of being inclusive; and they would never let this infect the minds of the youngest members of the society.

All of this was conveyed to our teacher with dignity and courtesy. Would he want to see himself as a man of knowledge to whom the future of the country could be entrusted, he was asked. Our teacher stood silent, thinking. Then finally he spoke. Yes, he acknowledged, he had tried to separate the two boys. And no, he had not bothered to think through the consequences of his actions when he did so. This was the way he had seen society being structured around him always, and he was just blindly following the rules. No one had ever taught him otherwise, or made him see the futility of such divisions. He promised to rectify the wrong he had done the very next day. And he did do so.

This was how I had a first-hand experience of the way the three religious elders settled a matter firmly and openly. They made the problem go away without letting it grow and fester— the essence of good management in any situation, I later learnt.

It was also the first glimmer of a thought that has shaped me since: that it must always be our inner convictions and strength of beliefs that dictate our actions. External forces, temptations and counsels will always be dinned into us, but those among us who can stand up to what we innately believe to be good and right will finally be at peace with ourselves. Our country needs citizens who trust their individuality, who cannot be manipulated by people with unscrupulous agendas.

As far as the fact of my religion is concerned, from Rameswaram I followed my destiny that took me into the world of science and technology. I was always a believer in science, but the spiritual atmosphere of my youth has stayed with me. I well understand different points of view, particularly about God. I have read and assimilated the knowledge contained in different religious texts—from the Koran to the Gita to the Holy Bible. Together they have made me a product of this unique land of ours, a syncretic creation of the best of our diverse traditions. And if ever I am asked what it is like to be a Muslim in this country, I can point to the people I grew up with—my father, Sastrygal and Father Bodal, indeed many others like them whom I met later—who have upheld the religious and moral standards of our nation. In their own ways they have contributed to make ours a country we can justly proclaim to be a multi-religious, multi-ethnic nation, where there is space for each of us to breathe. Yes, we have deep problems and fissures being created daily, but if the generations to come remember the stories of people like my great-great-grandfather and the imam and priests of the Rameswaram of long ago, I am sure we will continue to survive and thrive as a secular democracy forever.

my mother and my sister

M any years ago, I wrote a poem called 'My Mother', which began with these lines:

Sea waves, golden sand, pilgrims' faith,
Rameswaram Mosque Street, all merge into one,
My Mother!

My growing up years, which I now remember with such nostalgia, are suffused with the memory of Rameswaram, and the two people who were the centre of my world then—my father and mother. Ours was a middle-class family. My father had his own small business besides being the imam of the mosque. My mother, Ashiamma, came from a family, one of whom had some time in the past been given the title of 'Bahadur' by the British.

My mother was a gentle, down-to-earth, pious woman. She was a devout Muslim, like my father, and when I think of her I cannot but remember her saying her namaz five times a day, bending and praying, the look on her face one of extreme devotion and peacefulness. She had a large family to look after and that was where most of her energy went. Our family consisted of my siblings and I, as well as our relatives, like my grandparents and my uncles, all of who lived in the same house. Providing for everyone was always a stretch on the resources. It was not a time of plenty for anyone, least of all for us. We had a good steady income from my father's businesses—his coconut groves and ferry business—but that just about covered our expenses, and there was never any question about indulging in luxuries.

In these circumstances, my mother remained the ideal partner for my father. She saved and understood frugality, yet there was never a trace of irritation or anger in her about the way of life that we led. Almost daily, not only were the many members of the family fed and looked after satisfactorily, we usually had umpteen people drop by who would be told to stay back and eat with us. Now that I think about it, I feel that she cooked and served for as many—if not more—guests as there were members of the household. Yet, this was accepted as normal, and no one really remarked on it or thought much about it. Such was the Indian concept of hospitality once upon a time.

Mine was a happy, secure childhood. One of my earliest memories is of eating with my mother, sitting on the kitchen floor. We ate off banana leaves. Rice, aromatic sambar, home-made pickles and coconut chutney were the staple foods. Her cooking was deceptively simple and till today, I have not eaten sambar that balances the tart and the spicy tastes as delicately as hers did. It is again in connection with food that another anecdote from my childhood comes to me.

During the World War II years, food was being rationed and there was a general shortage of nearly everything. My mother and grandmother did their best to tide over those days, stretching the supplies as much as they could, cutting out any wastage, often reducing the portions on their plates so that the children had enough to eat. One day, my mother had made chapattis instead of rice. I sat at my place on the floor and ate with great relish as she rolled out one fresh chapatti after another. They kept coming and I kept eating. I was a hungry little boy after all. When I had finally had my fill, I picked up my banana leaf plate and walked away to wash up. Later that night, my elder brother took me aside and scolded me for the first time. 'How could you be so blind, Abdul?' he started.

At first I had no idea why I was being pulled up. I stared uncomprehendingly at him. Then he softened and explained, 'Did you not notice that there is just enough for all of us to eat two–three chapattis each? Amma will never say no to you, but because you kept eating, she kept serving you, and tonight she will go hungry, because now there is nothing left for her to eat.'

That moment of shame, of heartbreak for my beloved mother, who looked frail, yet was the toughest woman I knew, broke my heart. I cried to myself, too mortified to show my face to anyone, and it was only after a few days that I could bring myself to look her in the face again. What a lesson that was for me to never forget the needs of those around me! Her love drove her to share her food with me without a second thought, and after my brother showed me the truth, I could never again eat without making sure there was enough to go around—especially for my mother and grandmother.

I left home fairly early in life, as I wanted to pursue my studies in a different, larger town. As a result, I could not remain my mother's little boy for too long, unlike many of my friends. But her generosity and caring spirit stayed in my heart always.

Again, during the World War II years, when I was about eight years old, I have described how I took the job of a newspaper delivery boy. My day began well before dawn, when I had to go for my tuitions, my Koran class, do my newspaper rounds, go to school and then return home well into the evening, when I had to study for the next day. In all this, my mother stood by me like a rock. Early in the morning, she would wake up well before me, draw the water for my bath and then call me. My mother saw me off and would be waiting for me to come back an hour or two later, when I would have to go with my father to the Arabic School for my Holy Koran lessons. As I went from place to place during the daytime, all I had time for were the meals that would be laid out for me promptly. I knew that many times my mother decreased her own share so that I could have enough. When I once questioned her, she only smiled and said, 'You are a growing child. You have so much to do all through the day. This is what mothers look out for, don't worry about me.' In the evenings when I returned home hungry and tired, she would again help me clean up and prepare for the next day.

Among all my siblings, I was always given precedence in taking a place by her. Once, I remember I fell asleep with my head in her lap. She sat quietly, her hands softly caressing my hair and cheeks, her touch the most precious balm for my tiredness. Unknown to me, from somewhere deep within, tears sprang up in my heart. Before I could stop them, they started flowing down. My eyes were still closed, yet the tears ran. They dropped on to my folded knees and seeped into my mother's sari. But she did not stop her caresses. She knew exactly what was giving rise to those tears—the extreme tiredness of a boy suddenly trying to be a man. Her fingers ran tenderly through my hair, comforting, soothing and understanding.

This simple lady, born and raised in a small southern Indian town, was perhaps like many other mothers in our land and beyond. She did not step out of the house and take part in the affairs of the town. She did not make a career in the way we think of it nowadays. Her realm of work remained the home and the family. Yet, within that, she served everyone and God with utmost devotion, selflessness and piety. It is this lesson that I have carried from her life—that it does not matter how large or small your sphere of activity is, what counts finally is the commitment that you bring to the job that has been ordained for you in this life.

My father lived to the age of 102. When he passed away, he left behind a family that included fifteen grandchildren. His passing away affected me deeply. I came home from my work at Thumba and sat by my mother for a long time. When I had to leave, she blessed me in a choked voice. I was in the thick of building the SLV-3 rocket, and work beckoned me. She never once asked me to stay back. Should I have done so? Should I not have been so preoccupied with my work, and instead spent time with this old lady, who I was never to see again? I have asked myself this, and do not have an answer. My mother passed away soon after my father did. It was perhaps fitting that she would not live long alone, without the man whose side she had never left for over eighty years.

After I received the news of her passing, as I made my way to Rameswaram, memories of her assailed me. The two people who had created me, not just as their child, but moulded my thoughts and personality, were now no more. I would have to live out the rest of my life without their guidance. But I knew one could not have lived long without the other, and that is what comforted me as I returned to the mosque where I had learnt to pray with my father. The azaan from that mosque once used to bring all of us together—our parents leading all the children in the prayers. Now it is a sweet reminder of a beautiful childhood, of parents lost to time, of a mother who understood her boy's deepest feelings, even if they remained buried in his heart.

◆

My Sister Zohra

Ours was a large family and I was one of ten siblings. Besides my own brothers and sisters, cousins and children of distant relatives were always present in the house and we grew up never knowing the meaning of boredom. There was always a tree to climb, a game to play or an excursion to plan. We were a happy bunch of children—squabbling and then making up, sometimes being naughty and always ready to help each other out.

My sister, Zohra, was one of the older children. She grew up as many girls in her circumstances did. She went to school and studied, but she was also expected to help as much as possible around the house. In fact, she was perhaps my mother's closest companion. The bond of mother and daughter changed into that of friendship as they toiled for the family, cooking and cleaning, looking after the young ones, tending to their scraped knees and dripping noses. Like my mother, she, too, had a soft spot for me. It was perhaps because I was a bit of a dreamer even then. I was not as boisterous as my companions, and often preferred to curl up with a paper or a book, rather than plan a prank with the other boys. Zohra looked out for me as much as she could so that the soft innocence of her little brother was not destroyed.

When I was quite young, a cousin called Ahmed Jalalluddin entered our lives. He came like a breath of fresh air to the tiny community. He had studied up to middle grade, could read and write English, and more than that, his vision of life was open and large, ready to look beyond the shores of Rameswaram.

He stayed close by and became a part of the daily life of the family very quickly.

Jalalluddin took a great liking to me. He indulged my curiosities and did his best to find answers to the questions I asked. I was always full of questions about the things I saw around me—why do birds fly, how is rain created, how do train engines work and many more such things. Jalalluddin recognized the fact that I would soon outgrow the school in Rameswaram. He discussed with my father the need to send me to Ramanathapuram, where there was a bigger, better school.

My life took its course, and after completing my schooling at Ramanathapuram, I decided to move to Madras (now Chennai) to study engineering at the Madras Institute of Technology (MIT). In the intervening years, Zohra had married Jalalluddin. The two of them were the biggest supporters of my dreams and ambitions. Zohra was determined that I give wings to my aspirations and Jalalluddin remained my mentor. Yet, our financial situation remained the same. Our household was still dependent on the earnings from the businesses started by my father. How could they afford to pay the sum of ₹600 that was the admission fee at MIT? While today this may seem like a very small amount, at the time, for us, it was equivalent to nearly a lakh rupees.

That was when I saw the true grit in my sister. Nothing would stop her little brother, she told her husband. My parents had saved and got some pieces of gold jewellery made for her. Traditionally, in Indian households, the women may wear the jewellery on certain occasions, but many also use them as a safeguard—a kind of insurance policy for rainy days when there are unexpected cash requirements. Without a moment's further thought, and not worrying that the jewellery may one day be needed for her own family, for she was now a married woman, Zohra announced that she would use the pieces as guarantee with a moneylender and borrow the sum required for my admission.

I was deeply touched by her gesture. It was one of the most selfless things anyone had ever done for me. At the time of need Zohra had the solution to the problem, and she gave what she could with a full heart. She knew that her brother would work hard. She kept faith in my abilities—that I would qualify as an engineer. Her gold bangles and chain were mortgaged, the money came and I was admitted to MIT. I vowed at the time to release her jewellery from mortgage as soon as I started earning. I eventually did do so by studying hard and earning a scholarship.

Like my mother, Zohra lived out her life in Rameswaram.

She was as efficient, cheerful and upright as her and the two of them together symbolize for me the resilience and resourcefulness of the ordinary Indian woman. This woman is a person who cannot be cowed down too long by her circumstances. Often, she goes through life without recognizing her own dreams and ambitions. Many times she thinks of the ambitions of her husband, or the welfare and progress of her children. She will think of her father, brothers, sisters first and place herself behind everyone else. Where are her own dreams, I wonder? Destiny, tradition, situations will test her again and again. She will have to worry and compromise, save and innovate. Yet, she will find a way to guide her family and her dear ones out of any crisis, and she will do so with such love that it will inundate your heart.

my first mentor:
ahmed jalalluddin

A few remarkable people have appeared at critical times in my life and proceeded to mould or reorient my ways of thinking; sometimes they have even changed the course of my life. To these mentors I am always grateful and remember them more and more each day. Now, if I could have all the time in the world, I know what I would do; I would spend time in remembering these people who shaped my life. They are like the sun that warms the face and the winds that embrace. One such person in my life was Ahmed Jalalluddin.

When I was still a young boy, my father decided to build a boat to start a ferry business. I was fascinated with the way the boat was taking shape. As each plank of wood was slotted into its place and the outline of the boat became clearer, I found it harder and harder to tear myself away from that place by the beach where the boat was being built. Jalalluddin, who also lived in Rameswaram and would help my father, was the first to notice my interest in the boat. Unlike the other adults, who were too busy going about their work, he would spend some time chatting with me every day. We would talk about the boat, how it should be built and painted and all the work that still needed to get done on it. From there an unusual friendship grew between me—a little boy—and Jalalluddin—a much older, wiser person, who was fifteen years senior to me.

Our conversations gradually took other turns. As days turned into years and both of us grew older, Jalalluddin became my brother-in-law—he married my sister Zohra. Our relationship took on more depth. What I remember most distinctly from the time are our walks around Rameswaram town. We would set out almost every evening starting from Mosque Street, where our house was located, and walk towards the shore of the sea. The town would be busy at the time, with pilgrims making their way to and from the temple. Our first halt would be the Shiva temple, where our steps would fall in with those making their circumambulations. As they said their prayers, some would be kneeling and touching the ground after every few steps, while others would be helping old parents or relatives perform the pilgrimage. Amongst these people, our thoughts, too, would turn towards spiritual matters, and our conversation would often be about God.

Jalalluddin's relationship with God was slightly different from the one I was used to seeing in my father. My father was a pious man who followed every rule of worship—not just outwardly but as a deeply felt need within him. Saying the namaz and every other form of prayer was as much a part of his being as breathing or eating. Jalalluddin, too, was a devout man. However, for him, God was almost like a friend. He talked to God, and presented all his problems to Him in the way one does to a living entity. For him, it was inconceivable that God would not present a solution if Jalalluddin spoke about his dilemmas to Him. As we made our way with the pilgrims and I watched them perform their rituals, and listened to Jalalluddin at the same time, in my mind these two faiths melded into one. Was it possible that in this serene atmosphere of Rameswaram the prayers of so many of the faithful, uttered in different tongues and born from various beliefs, were reaching different gods? It could not be. I was convinced that the one who heard everyone out was a common entity. But I also secretly wondered if my friend had a special connection that allowed him to see God everywhere, and it was that which let him speak so freely to Him.

Jalalluddin was not very highly educated. He had been able to complete his education till the eighth standard only, as he had had to start working in order to earn for his family. But he was also among the few in Rameswaram with some knowledge of the English language. He could read and write English, and therefore, was in great demand among the residents to write their applications or any other official letters. Seeing the respect with which he was treated by the townspeople, I too wanted to be like him and study as much as possible. On his part, perhaps it was because of his slightly better educational background that Jalalluddin was among the first people to notice the immense curiosity and thirst for knowledge that flowed within me. In those days I had an insatiable interest to learn more about everything, and it was my brother-in-law who indulged my questions. I plied him with more and more queries and he would answer me as patiently as he could and with as much knowledge as he had gathered. He opened my eyes when he talked about so many things that lay outside the purview of our daily lives—nature, space, scientific discoveries, books and famous people.

I have often pondered the question: what creates our personalities? How much does the environment play a part and how much of it is inborn? If I look back at my life, I can put a finger on specific qualities that were transmitted to me from those closest to me. From my parents I learnt honesty, self-discipline, faith and kindness. And from my closest friends—Jalalluddin and my other cousin, Samsuddin—I learnt to recognize the fact that every human carries something special within himself. These men were the ones who saw a spark in me and encouraged and nurtured me. They were not sophisticated; rather, they had a direct, intuitive approach to life. They often knew my questions and ambitions even before I had been able to articulate them to my own self. They could then draw these out from within me and help me set my life's goals.

As I grew up, Jalalluddin was among the first to encourage me to break away from the confines of Rameswaram. When I wanted to continue my studies in a bigger school in a different town, he was the one who made the arrangements, travelled with me to Ramanathapuram and saw me settled into the Schwartz High School there. For a boy who had not known life outside the place where I had grown up, even Ramanathapuram was a big change. I missed my family, my familiar surroundings, my mother and her cooking. At that time it was Jalalluddin who instilled in me the power of positive thinking. He would tell me that I needed to control these emotions in order to fulfil my desires for a better education. Whenever I felt homesick and sad, I thought of him and his words, and they gave me the courage I needed to plunge into the unfamiliar life of a pupil living in a boarding school.

At every stage of my life, till I became an adult in the real sense of the word—someone who is in control of his own actions—this man walked with me. He picked me up when I faltered, encouraged me when I felt I could not carry on and stood by me as I took my first tentative steps in the outside world. How can I forget the day when he and Samsuddin accompanied me to Bombay (now Mumbai), to Santa Cruz airport, because I was going to do something no one had imagined even twenty years earlier in Rameswaram—I was going to the US, to NASA, on a six-month training programme. I had become an engineer by then and had been accepted as a rocket engineer by the Indian National Committee for Space Research (INCOSPAR) who were sending me to the United States.

Jalalluddin and Samsuddin saw me off at Santa Cruz airport. My trepidation about travelling abroad was reflected in their anxiety about being in a big city like Bombay. Yet, they carried their dignity upon them like a mantle. I recall seeing them at the airport gate, and feeling their positivity and optimism reach me in waves. They were men who saw only the good in me and had implicit faith in my following the correct path always. Standing there, I was overcome by my sentiments and my love for them and tears filled my eyes. Through the mist of the tears I held on to them, and Jalalluddin said to me, 'Abdul, we have always loved you, and we believe in you. We shall always be proud of you.' How can I ever forget those words of encouragement?

I now think that Jalalluddin not only held my hands and

taught me to walk tall in this world, he also taught me how to live. I grew into a man with my own ideas and creative thought processes under his influence—an influence that remained with me even when I moved far away from him and my family, and made my way in the world. And, if he taught me the ways of life, how could it be that he would not teach me the harshest, yet most constant fact of life—death.

While I was working on the SLV-3 rocket project for the Indian Space Research Organisation (ISRO), news came to me one day that my brother-in-law, my friend and guide, was no more. It was a deep shock for me. Jalalluddin was not of the age for this. When I got the news I was dumbstruck. How could this have happened? How could we all be alive, and this man be no more? In my shock I remember speaking words that made little sense. I could not think, feel or move for a time. Finally I gathered myself together, and leaving instructions with my colleague, I made preparations to leave for Rameswaram.

As I travelled back home, in buses that wheezed and groaned on the inter-city roads, buffeted by people and the wind blowing in from the open windows, amidst the chatter of fellow travellers, I felt myself to be completely alone. Perhaps there comes a time in each of our lives when we finally leave our childhood selves behind—and this was mine. With Jalalluddin, a part of me also passed away. Gone forever was the boy who needed to be guided, who asked questions by the dozen and who knew that whatever he did, there was a pair of loving hands always ready to hold his own hands and guide him. When I closed my eyes, images from long ago flashed by—of leaving for Ramanathapuram, of Jalalluddin arranging the money to buy my books, of him standing at Santa Cruz airport, tears glistening in his eyes—tears of unbearable pride that can be felt only by those who have truly loved and brought up a child. I saw him walking with me on the sandy shores of our little town, pointing out the stars and the moon, explaining where the sun went when it finally sank into the sea.

I reached home to find my sister grieving piteously. With her was my little niece Mehboob, her father gone well before his time. I met my father, who was now a hundred years old, and yet, for the first time, I felt that he had really aged. The grief of losing his son-in-law seemed to have shifted something within him. We put our dear friend and son to rest. And the whole time I could not find the tears to shed at his going. It was as if I was walking in a daze, through a fog of memories.

After the burial, my father, that most perceptive of men even in his great old age, held my hands and sat me beside him. For the first time I noticed that he, too, had not shed tears. He said to me, 'Abdul, do you not see how the Lord strengthens the shadows? Had it been His will, He could have made them constant. But He makes the sun their guide, little by little He shortens them. He has made the night for us to rest, and has sent Jalalluddin into a long sleep—a dreamless sleep, a complete rest of all his being within simple unconsciousness. Nothing happens that has not been ordained by Allah and in Him we will have to keep our trust and faith.'

I sat back and reflected on my father's wise words. Death is not something to be afraid of, and I have never seen it that way. Yet, the sadness that it brings cannot be shrugged away. We will go when our time will come, but when some of us go earlier than the others, like Jalalluddin, who did not live to see his children grow into adults, who did not get to see them married or played with his grandchildren, the sadness that wells up within the heart is a reality that one has to go on living with.

My friend Ahmed Jalalluddin was an ordinary man for many. But my friend and mentor Ahmed Jalalluddin was also a remarkable man. He brought about change and shaped the minds of those around him with the sheer power of his love, simplicity and understanding. There are such remarkable men in every city and village in this country. I was lucky that I found him so near to me and that he chose to grasp my hands when he did in order to make me the man I would become one day.

when i failed

In my life, which has been long and eventful, I have seen great heights of success. I have been part of ventures that have contributed to the growth of our nation in the field of science and technology; I have also had the privilege of occupying the highest office in the country. There are many achievements to look back upon—some of my own doing and some where I had the privilege to be part of teams, which were immensely talented. Yet, I firmly believe that unless one has tasted the bitter pill of failure, one cannot aspire enough for success. I have seen both sides of the coin and have learnt life's toughest lessons when I have stared into the pit of despair that failure brings with it. These lessons are well worth recounting and remembering, as they have helped me work my way through many difficult situations.

One of the earliest such episodes from my life happened when I was a student of aeronautics at MIT. My design teacher there was Professor Srinivasan, who was also the head of the institute. Once, we were placed in teams of four students each, and our team had to design a low-level attack aircraft. I was in charge of coming up with the aerodynamic design. We worked very hard for weeks. My teammates were designing all the other components, like the propulsion, structure, control and instrumentation. Since our other course work was over at the time, we spent long hours discussing our ideas and researching them. We were all keen to impress our professors with our project. They kept an eye on the progress and after a few days, Professor Srinivasan asked to see the design I had created. When I showed it to him, he examined it with his characteristic critical eye. I stood by, waiting with bated breath to hear his verdict. I still remember the way his eyebrows crinkled as he looked at the paper spread out in front of him. Then he straightened up and his next words stunned me. 'This is just not good enough, Kalam,' he said. He turned stern eyes on me and continued, 'I expected much better from you. This is dismal work and I am disappointed that someone with your talent has come up with work like this.' I stared at the professor, dumbfounded. I had always been the star pupil in any class and had never ever been pulled up by a teacher for anything. This feeling of embarrassment and shame was a new experience for me, and I did not like it one bit. The professor shook his head some more and told me that I had to redo the entire design, starting from scratch and rethinking all my assumptions. I agreed shamefacedly. Then he broke the next bad news. Not only was I supposed to do the work again, I had to finish it in three days! 'Today is Friday afternoon, young man. I want to see a flawless configuration drawing by Monday evening. If you are unable to do so, your scholarship will be stopped.' I was even more dumbfounded now. The scholarship was the only way I could afford to be in college. Without it I would have to stop my studies. My own ambitions, the dreams of my parents, my sister and Jalalluddin flashed before my eyes and seemed to recede to a distance. It was unthinkable that the future could turn so bleak with a few words spoken by my professor.

I got to work right away, determined to prove myself. I skipped dinner and remained at the drawing board through the night. Where earlier the components of my design were floating in my head, now they suddenly came together and took on forms and shapes I could work with. The concentrated work I put in seemed to brush away all the cobwebs of the mind. By the next morning, I was working like a man possessed. I took a short break to eat and freshen up, and went back to work again. By Sunday evening, my work was nearly complete—an elegant, neat design that I was proud of. While I was putting my final touches to it, I sensed a presence in the room. It was the professor, still dressed in his tennis whites, on his way back from the club. I didn't know how long he had been standing there, watching me. Now, as our eyes met, he came forward. He looked critically at my work for many minutes. Then he straightened up and smiled. To my amazement, he hugged me affectionately. Then patting me on the back, he said, 'I knew I was putting you under immense pressure when I rejected your work the other day. I set an impossible deadline—yet you have met it with work that I can only call outstanding. As your teacher, I had to push you to your limits so that you could recognize your own true potential.' After two days of extreme dejection, those words were music to my ears and revived my confidence and self-belief.

That day I learnt two lessons: a teacher who has his or her student's progress in mind is the best possible friend, because the teacher knows how to make sure that you excel. And second, there is no such thing as an impossible deadline. I have worked on many tough assignments, some of which had the country's top leaders watching over my work, but the assurance I gained in my capabilities at MIT thanks to Professor Srinivasan, helped me later in life too.

After MIT, I started my working life. Little did I know that even tougher lessons were to follow. I went to work at Hindustan Aeronautics Limited (HAL) in Bangalore. There I learnt a lot about aircraft and their design and technology. By now I was very sure that I wanted a career in flying. When I emerged as a graduate aeronautical engineer from HAL, I got two job opportunities. One was in the air force and another at the Directorate of Technical Development and Production (DTD&P [Air]) at the Ministry of Defence. I received interview calls from both. The first was in Dehra Dun and the second in Delhi. I set forth with great hope in my heart.

My first close sight of an aircraft had been at MIT, where two decommissioned aircraft were kept for the demonstration of various subsystems to the students. They had held a special fascination for me, and I was drawn to them again and again. They represented for me man's ability to think beyond his boundaries, and to give wings to dreams. I had chosen aeronautical engineering as my area of study because of my fascination for flying. Over the years I had nurtured the hope to be able to fly; to handle a machine as it rose higher and higher in the stratosphere was my dearest dream.

As I made my way from Madras to north India for the interviews, I played this dream over and over again in my mind. I was finally on the threshold of becoming a pilot! The journey from Tamil Nadu to Dehra Dun was a long one—not just geographically but also in terms of the distance I would travel from my humble origins to the prize that lay in the foothills of the Himalayas—a place in the air force as a pilot.

I first halted in Delhi for my interview at DTD&P. I was confident and the interview was an easy one, not requiring me to push the boundaries of my knowledge too far. I spent a week in Delhi and then proceeded to Dehra Dun for my interview at the Air Force Selection Board. Here, I should mention that at the time, as a young man in my early twenties, I was just beginning to understand how to conduct myself in the wider world. When I had first moved from Rameswaram to the bigger cities for my studies, I was a shy, tongue-tied boy. I had to work hard to develop some assertiveness in my personality. I did this by trying to communicate with different people from all kinds of backgrounds. It was not easy and there were many moments of frustration and disappointment. However, by the time I finished my studies and headed out to look for a job, my personality was better developed and I was able to articulate my thoughts well enough in English and Tamil.

To return to my interview at the Air Force Selection Board, as I started answering the queries put forth to me, I realized that along with qualifications and engineering knowledge, they were also looking for a certain kind of 'smartness' in the candidate. Physical fitness and an articulate manner were what they were seeking. I gave it my best. I had wanted this job for so long and so deeply that I was determined yet anxious, confident and at the same time tense. Finally the results were announced. I had stood ninth in a batch of twenty-five. There were only eight places available. I had failed to realize my dream of becoming an air force pilot.

I still remember the ache in my heart as I attempted to make sense of what had happened. When a dearly held desire begins to break up, one can feel nothing but despair and emptiness as one tries to come to terms with the end of a dream. I could not bear to be indoors after seeing the result. I had to go out for air and be in the open, because all around me the walls seemed to close in. I walked around for a while till I reached the edge of a cliff. I stood there looking down at the shimmering waters of a lake and wondered what I should do next. Plans needed to be changed and priorities reassessed. I decided to go to Rishikesh for a few days and seek a new way forward.

I reached Rishikesh the next morning. I took a dip in the Ganga—a river I had heard so much about, but was seeing and experiencing for the first time in my life. I had been told about the Sivananda Ashram that was located a little way up a hill. I walked there. As I entered I felt a strange vibration, a sense of tranquility that was like a balm for my restless soul. Sadhus were seated all around, deep in meditation. I hoped that one among them would be able to answer the questions that troubled me and soothe my worries. I was granted an audience with Swami Sivananda himself. My being a Muslim did not affect him in any way. Instead, before I could speak, he asked what had filled me with sorrow. I only fleetingly wondered how he knew about my sadness before I embarked on an explanation of the recent developments in my life. He listened calmly and then washed away my anxieties with a smile of deep peacefulness. His next words were some of the most profound I had ever heard. His feeble yet deep voice still resonates when I think of them:

'Accept your destiny and go ahead with your life. You are not destined to become an air force pilot. What you are destined to become is not revealed now but it is predetermined. Forget this failure, as it was essential to lead you to your destined path. Search, instead, for the true purpose of your existence... Surrender yourself to the wish of God.'

That lesson made a deep impression on my mind. Truly, why fight against destiny? This failure, I was sure, was part of a larger plan that God had for me. I ruminated long about this as I went back to Delhi. There, I found that I had been accepted as senior scientific assistant at DTD&P. I gave up my dream of making a career out of flying. I understood now that there was plenty of other work to be done, and I was going to put my heart and soul into the job that had been given to me.

In this way I started my working life. Like me, I am sure almost every person who sets out with a goal has had to face unexpected obstacles. We've had to rethink our goals, reorient our paths. Each setback teaches us a new facet of life and something about our own personalities. When we tackle obstacles, we find hidden reserves of courage and resilience we did not know we had. And it is only when we are faced with failure do we realize that these resources were always there within us. We only need to find them and move on with our lives.

my favourite books

Whenever I talk to the youth anywhere in India, I am invariably asked one question: which are your favourite books? Even though modern life has changed many of our habits, reading is one activity that is still popular in our country. From newspapers and magazines to books, there is no dearth of reading matter available to us. It is heartening that with the growth of the literacy rate in India, the demand for books of different kinds has grown. This shows, I think, that people are not just learning to read and write in school. They are also getting educated and improving their ways of thinking and sharpening their powers of understanding. Reading helps to build these invaluable qualities and the habit of reading can never be encouraged enough.

For me personally, books have always been close companions. I discovered some when I was very young, and have never forgotten them. They are like friends who have led me by the hand and guided me through life. Their words breathe meaning into many situations, for I use them to understand the world around me.

I have also come across many book lovers who have fanned my love of books. One person in particular who helped me out once by *not* buying a book comes to mind. This happened in Madras many years back, when I was studying at MIT. I had recently become interested in Russian literature, and had obtained a copy of a book that I was reading with great interest. However, it so happened that I also needed to go home for a few days and as always there was hardly any money in my pocket—not enough to buy a train ticket even for Rameswaram! I saw no way out other than selling the book I was reading in order to tide over this monetary crisis. The place where I went for all such transactions was called More Market in Madras. It was a covered shopping area where all manner of goods were available. But what interested me most was a narrow area towards the rear where second-hand books were bought and sold. There was one shop which I always visited, as the proprietor had become a friend. He had introduced me to many writers and helped me become a voracious reader by providing me with many interesting and uplifting books. That day, when I presented myself at his shop and told him that I needed to sell the book I was reading, he looked at me with a mixture of pity and sadness. He could see that I did not want to part with the book, yet he also understood my reason for wanting to do so. Then he came up with an idea that was brilliant in its simplicity and solved all my problems! Why didn't I leave the book with him as a sort of mortgage? He would loan me the amount he would have paid me for it. When I had the money I could return the amount to him and take back my book. He promised not to sell it to anyone in the meantime! My happiness knew no bounds at this sudden change in my fortunes. I was now able to go home and not lose my book. Needless to say, my book-loving friend kept his word, and that book stayed with me for many years—a reminder of the kindness of strangers and the equally strange world of bibliophiles!

I started reading the English classics only when I was in my final year at St Joseph's College. At the time, I discovered the works of Leo Tolstoy, Walter Scott and Thomas Hardy. The settings of the stories were completely alien to me, and the language different from what I was used to, but the stories of human relationships and their views of society appealed to me. After this I discovered the works of certain philosophers and started taking an interest in reading about science, in particular physics.

Here, I am reminded of a story about Albert Einstein. When he was twelve, his mentor, Max Talmud, gave him a book on Eucledian geometry. This book opened the young Einstein's mind to concepts of pure thought and how to explore universal truths, and he began to realize the power of the human mind.

Over the years I have read innumerable books. But if I were asked to name those that are most dear to me, or the ones that affected me deeply, I would mention three.

The first is called *Light from Many Lamps,* edited by Lillian Eichler Watson. I first came across this book in 1953, in the very same second-hand bookstore in Madras I had mentioned earlier (the joys of browsing in a crammed bookshop and stumbling upon a rare treasure like this is indescribable). I consider the book to be my companion, because I have leafed through it and read and reread it so many times over the years that I have possessed it. Considered a classic inspirational work, *Lights from Many Lamps* contains the writings of various authors. The editor has compiled inspiring stories written by different writers, and has also, very helpfully, mentioned how these came to be written and the lessons to be derived from them.

There has hardly been an occasion when the works mentioned in the book have not brought me solace in my hours of sadness, or uplifted me when I needed advice. If I am ever in danger of being swept away by my own emotions, this book brings about a balance in my thinking. My copy of the book has been bound and rebound so many times that I was delighted when a friend found a new edition and gifted it to me some years ago.

The second work that has been influential in my thinking is the *Thirukural*. Written by Thiruvalluvar more than 2,000 years ago, it is a collection of 1,330 rhyming Tamil couplets or aphorisms (*kural*). This work talks about almost every aspect of life and is considered to be one of the most important pieces of work in Tamil literature. To me, it has provided a code of conduct for my life. It is a work that truly elevates the mind. Here is a *kural* that is particularly dear to my heart:

Ulluvathellam uyarvullal matratu
Tallinum tellamai nirttut
(Think of rising higher. Let it be your only thought.
Even if your object be not attained, the thought itself
will have raised you.)

The next book that I would like to mention is called *Man the Unknown* by the Nobel laureate and doctor-turned-philosopher Alexis Carrel. In it, he talks about how humans can be healed when both the body and mind are treated together. His description of the human body—how it is an intelligent, integrated system—is explained clearly and brilliantly. I think this work should be read by everyone, in particular those who aim to study the medical sciences.

Religious texts of different religions have influenced me greatly. I have studied these and tried to find the answers to questions that have appeared in my mind through my life. The Koran, the Vedas, the Bhagwad Gita, all hold deep philosophical insights into the plight of man and have helped me resolve many dilemmas at different times in my life.

Just to illustrate how these texts can provide insight into any aspect of life, let me recount a few examples. After I had worked for a while as an aeronautical engineer in Bangalore, I was called for an interview for the post of rocket engineer at INCOSPAR, the space agency started by Dr Vikram Sarabhai. I was very nervous about the interview and did not know what to expect. At the time, these words by Lakshmana Sastry (my father's friend and the priest at the Rameswaram temple) quoting the Gita gave me courage: 'All beings are born to delusion... overcome by the dualities that arise from wish and hate...but those men of virtuous deeds in whom sin has come to an end, freed from the delusion of dualities, worship me steadfast in their vows.' I told myself the best way to win was not to need to win and I went for the interview with this attitude.

India's space programme grew and with it, I got to work with many people who helped build it and give it shape. My connection with the Indian Space Research Organisation goes back right to the time of its inception. When I look at the way the organization has grown and the kind of service it has provided our country, as well as the people who shaped its objectives and gave it direction, I am reminded of a *shloka* from the Gita which says: 'See the flower, how generously it distributes perfume and honey. When its work is done, it falls away quietly. Try to be like the flower, unassuming despite all its qualities.' The stalwarts of the space programme were like these flowers—they came and gave direction and then made way for new ideas and new thoughts.

Again, while I was at the Defence Research and Development Organisation (DRDO) working on developing India's indigenous missile programme, I worked with many brilliant and dedicated engineers and leaders. The words from the Holy Koran ring in my ears when I think of them: 'Light upon light. Allah guides His light to whom He will.'

In my personal life too, these works have given me comfort and helped me make sense of the vicissitudes of life. When I lost my parents within the span of a year, I remember praying at the mosque in Rameswaram, overcome with grief and regret for not having met my mother more often before she passed away. But after some time this line from the Koran came to me. It told me that the passing away of souls is inevitable and the only constant is God: 'Your wealth and children are only a temptation whereas Allah! With Him is eternal award.'

Poetry has been one of my first loves in the realm of literature. The works of T.S. Eliot, Lewis Carroll and William Butler Yeats have played out in my mind over and over again, appearing to give context and meaning to various happenings. In my endeavours in the scientific arena, how appropriate have been these lines by Lewis Carroll:

Let craft, ambition, spite,
Be quenched in Reason's night,
Till weakness turn to might,
Till what is dark be light,
Till what is wrong be right!

And when work was an endless cycle of back-breaking hours, and days merged into days till I could hardly tell one from the other, Samuel Taylor Coleridge's words described my state of mind the best:

Day after day, day after day,
We stuck, nor breath, nor motion;
As idle as a painted ship
Upon a painted ocean

Often, I have had to work trying to meet impossible deadlines. A colleague, Group Captain Narayanan, was impatient to achieve our goal of creating guided missiles. He told me once, 'You name the thing and I will get it for you, but do not ask me for time.' At the time I had laughed at his hurry and quoted these words by T.S. Eliot:

Between the conception
And the creation
Between the emotion
And the response
Falls the Shadow.

These are just some of the writers and works that have influenced me deeply. They are all like old friends—familiar, well-meaning and reassuring. They know when to enter my mind; they know when I am in some dilemma, or my moments of sadness and contemplation. They are also with me in my most deeply joyous moments. In this age of quick and easy communication, when information comes to us in byte-sized pieces, the charm of the written word can never be allowed to be lost. I once wrote this poem on books that I often read out to young people. It sums up my feelings for the written word:

Books were always my friends
Last more than fifty years
Books gave me dreams
Dreams resulted in missions
Books helped me confidently take up the missions
Books gave me courage at the time of failures
Good books were for me angels
Touched my heart gently at the time
Hence I ask young friends to have books as friends
Books are your good friends.

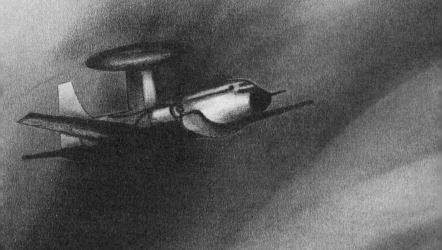

a brush with fire

have recounted in an earlier chapter some of my first experiences of dejection and failure and the lessons they held for me. I have understood now that after the feelings of disappointment subside, and one gains perspective, these experiences can change our ways of thinking. They also deeply impact our souls, I believe, and bring us face to face with existential issues. When that happens, we need to embrace the events and analyze how we responded—did we allow them to merely roll over us like waves, or did we dive deeper into the matter and use it to gain insights into ourselves?

Needless to say, it is usually events of great magnitude that shift something within us at a fundamental level. When we are unable to live up to the high standards and expectations of those we value the most; or get involved in matters that impact the lives of millions; or when it is a matter of life and death—these are the times when our sense of self and our ego witness deep changes.

I can recall a few such markers from my working life. When I was leading the project teams for SLV-3, the satellite launch vehicle, and for Agni, India's first indigenous missile, expectations from me and my teams were sky-high—both from the government and from the people of the country. The media scrutiny, though nothing compared to what it is today, was also intensive. SLV-3 failed on its first launch and the Agni project, too, went through numerous ups and downs and witnessed pre-launch difficulties. These were jobs that put the teams and me under immense pressure and the stakes were very high. Not getting these perfect the first time around negated the many other successes we had achieved despite various hurdles. Those days of introspection and analysis of the reasons for failure will remain deeply embedded in my memory. But what leaves an even greater impact is when people we know and work with, or those on whom we depend to implement our ideas and designs, show uncommon dedication and even suffer in the process. I have seen this, too, in my working life and each time I have been moved beyond words by what I witnessed.

In the 1960s and '70s, I was working at Thumba Equatorial Rocket Launching Station (TERLS). Under the guidance of Dr Vikram Sarabhai, we were making our own rockets, SLVs and satellites. We were also working with laboratories around the country in preparing payloads for the sounding rockets. Almost all physical laboratories in India were involved in the sounding rocket programme, each having its own mission and payload. These payloads were required to be integrated with the rocket structure. One of my colleagues at the Payload Preparation Laboratory was Sudhakar. Once, we were working on a pre-launch schedule, and were filling and remotely pressing a dangerous sodium and thermite mix. Like most days at Thumba, which is on the east coast, it was hot and humid. Sudhakar and I had been working for a long time. The heat was intense but we were unmindful of it. After filling six such mixes, we decided to visit the payload room and inspect the progress to see for ourselves if the mix had been filled properly. Perhaps, because we were so deeply immersed in our work, we forgot a basic fact of science: pure sodium, when in contact with water, can be dangerous. As Sudhakar and I leaned in to inspect the mixture, a drop of sweat from Sudhakar's forehead fell into it. Before we could react, we were thrown backwards by a powerful explosion! It shook the room and both of us fell. For a few seconds, the shock paralysed me. In a matter of seconds a fire broke out from the explosion. In front of our horrified eyes, the laboratory was soon burning away fiercely. It was a fire due to sodium, so using water would not help. Rather, it would add to the devastation. The laboratory was now nothing short of an inferno. Later, when I relived the events, it all seemed to take place in slow motion—the accident, the explosion and then the fire. In reality, all this happened within the space of a few seconds. Even as I got to my feet, Sudhakar showed a startling presence of mind. He broke open the glass window of the payload room with his bare hands. Then, without a moment's hesitation, he turned to me and pushed me out before proceeding to jump himself. These actions could not have taken more than a few minutes, yet if one considers the intensity of the explosion and the terrible heat of the fire, by the time it took Sudhakar to figure out our escape and save me, he himself got terribly injured. Not only was he severely burnt, but his hands were also bleeding from having broken the glass pane with no protection.

As we staggered away from the room that was now engulfed in flames, I held on to Sudhakar and thanked him for saving me. Despite the intense pain he was in, he smiled and acknowledged my words. He went on to spend many weeks in hospital recovering from his injuries. As for me, not only had I been in the most terrible accident of my life, I was also experiencing for the first time the feelings of a survivor. Knowing that someone willingly and instinctively put his life at risk in order to save yours is an incredibly humbling experience. People who have survived and been rescued from mortal danger face a gamut of emotions—from relief to guilt to gratitude. In my case it also came with a feeling of added responsibility. If Sudhakar had thought my life was worth saving without minding his own safety, then I needed more than ever to see that all the work we were doing together did not suffer an instant's delay.

Sudhakar's story of courage has been an abiding source of inspiration for me. Whenever I feel myself giving importance to the small issues of life, when I find myself losing sight of the larger picture, perhaps losing sight of the fact that I am just one in a humanity of billions and less than a speck in this universe, at those times I remember this incredible man. He looked like any other—a scientist like all of us going about his job—yet he rose above the most basic of fears, that of saving your own self, and did something extraordinary.

There is another incident that still leaves its painful imprint on my heart when I think about it. This was the Arakkonam crash of 1999. It left a deep well of sadness within me and altered my ego structure forever. Soon after it happened, I absorbed its importance but buried my feelings under a mountain of work. It was only years later, while talking to a close friend when we were writing a book together, that I could articulate my feelings and recount what had happened without sinking into regret and sadness.

On 11 January 1999, two aircraft took off from Bangalore towards the Arakkonam–Chennai coastline on a scientific mission for the Airborne Surveillance Platform (ASP). One was an Avro with an aircraft surveillance system mounted atop as a motodome (a dish-like structure fixed on the aircraft body). It climbed to 10,000 feet and set course for the coast where the radar testing was being carried out somewhere over the coastline. Fifteen minutes before the Avro took off, an AN-32 aircraft, which was the target aircraft for the radar testing, had also taken off from Bangalore. The testing happened for nearly one and half hours and everyone was happy with the performance of the radar system. The AN-32 landed at Arakkonam at around 4 p.m. The Avro ASP aircraft also set course towards Arakkonam at around this time. As it started its descent from 10,000 to 5,000 feet, all was well. But when the Avro was about 5 nautical miles away from the airfield, at an altitude somewhere between 3,000 and 5,000 feet, the motodome fell off. The sudden imbalance made the aircraft unstable and it crashed immediately. There were eight men on board. All of them died.

The news came to me when I was in the South Block, in a meeting of the Defence Research Council. I left midway and flew to Bangalore. Air Chief Marshal A.Y. Tipnis was also there. The days that followed were the most heart-rending. I met the bereaved families—the young wives, some with infants. What consolation could I offer them? That their beloved husbands and sons had died in the cause of defence preparedness? Is that of any solace to people when their worst fears have come true? I was speechless and shell-shocked when one young mother pointed to her baby and said, 'Who will look after this young life?' The mother of another asked me something that haunts me still, 'Why did you do this to us?'

The crash had been of such intensity that we could not locate any remains of the eight men. All we could do was prepare some coffins for the comfort of the families. We placed them in the air force hall and somehow I made a speech, bidding farewell to the eight men who had set out that afternoon to do their jobs, but never came home. I returned to my room that night exhausted and worn out with grief, worry and guilt. I wrote in my diary:

The lamps are different
But the light is same
Worldly joys you returned to the world
You remain in my innermost soul.

As years passed after this incident, I moved from my office at South Block to Rashtrapati Bhavan. But there, too, the cries of the widows, the grief of the devastated parents and the wailing of the infants remained with me. The fact that they did not even get to see the men for the last time and had to make do with symbolic coffins broke my heart when I thought about it. When grand plans for scientific and defence technologies are made, do the people in power think about the sacrifices the people in the laboratories and fields have to make? Political rhetoric alone does not build a nation unless it is backed by the power of sacrifice, toil and virtue. That is true nation-building.

When we obtain positions of power over others, we believe that we have reached the pinnacle of success. But it is at this time that we need to look back and be aware of the multitudes on whose hard work and sacrifices we have built our castles. When I was speaking to my friend, Arun Tiwari, about this episode, he asked me, 'What is the message?' My reply was, 'Don't pretend to be a candle, be a moth. Know the power hidden in serving. We seem to have got stuck with external forms of politics and mistaking them to be nation-building. It is sacrifices, toil and valour that are seldom seen that truly make a nation.'

Now, when I think back on these incidents, not only of their immediate impact but the events that unfolded subsequently—of Sudhakar in hospital, of the compensation that the families received from the government for their fallen men, but only after a long-drawn-out process—I feel a profound aloneness too. In sadness you are truly alone. That is when your true self is revealed to you, and I found myself reaching out to a larger consciousness, of the awareness that these questions about the nature of life and existence were triggering resolutions and giving birth to new depths of wisdom. Each one of us has to confront death and heartbreak in our lives, but if there is something I have learnt in my eight decades of life on this planet, it is that these moments are our true friends. Joy is fleeting, whereas true happiness and calm can come to us only after intense pain, when we have confronted ourselves in the mirror of our souls and understood the self.

my mentor:
dr vikram sarabhai

Teachers and mentors come at various stages into our lives. As a child, I looked up to my parents and my teachers. Then my dear friend and brother-in-law, Ahmed Jalalluddin, guided me in the crucial years when I turned from a child into a man. And as my career was beginning, I was immensely lucky to come in the orbit of a man such as Dr Vikram Sarabhai.

A scientist, educationist, institution builder and visionary, Dr Sarabhai was one of modern India's greatest thinkers and doers. He combined an acute intelligence with the qualities of a fine leader. It was the country's good fortune that he was chosen to helm its fledgling space programme after Independence. Much has been written about him and his many achievements—that he set up ISRO, articulated India's space mission, he was chairman of the Atomic Energy Commission and set up a number of other industries and educational institutions, not the least being the Indian Institute of Management (IIM), Ahmedabad. Yet, from where I saw him, he was all this—these were the stuff of legends and made him somewhat of a heroic figure for a young rocket engineer like me—and he was much more.

I first met him when I was called for an interview by INCOSPAR for the position of rocket engineer. The call for the interview had come to me quite unexpectedly, after Professor M.G.K. Menon of the Tata Institute of Fundamental Research (TIFR) saw my work on the Nandi hovercraft in Bangalore. I had little idea of what to expect at the interview, or who would be conducting it. Neither did I know exactly what areas of my knowledge the interviewers would test. I went to Bombay with an open mind, telling myself not to raise my expectations too much. Life had already taught me that the best way to win is to not covet the win too much, instead to keep a calm and open mind to new challenges.

I was interviewed by Dr Sarabhai, Professor Menon and Mr Saraf, who was the deputy secretary of the Atomic Energy Commission. Each one of them was a storehouse of scientific knowledge, yet the warmth and graciousness that I felt in the room was remarkable. That interview set the tone for my future relationship with Dr Vikram Sarabhai. He probed more into my thought processes, trying to not only find out my level of knowledge, but to know what I was made of as a person, where my goals lay and the possibilities for growth that I held within me, both as a professional and as a human being. He was encouraging, affable and listened to me in such a way that instinctively I knew that here was a man who was not recruiting just an engineer, rather he was looking at my future potential and was investing his time and care in me. In my professional life this was the first time that I had come across someone of his stature who seemed ready to envelop my thoughts and dreams into his larger vision for the country's space programme.

I was inducted into INCOSPAR. It was like a dream come true for me, and a great career breakthrough. As I settled down into my role and got to know the institution and its processes and people, I was struck by how different it was from where I had worked earlier. The atmosphere was much more relaxed, and labels and hierarchy were not as important.

Soon after this I heard the story of how Dr Sarabhai set up the Thumba Equatorial Rocket Launching Station. It is a story I never tire of telling, because to me it is the perfect coming together of science and spirituality—the twin driving forces of my life.

It was the year 1962 and Dr Vikram Sarabhai was looking for a site to establish a space research station. He visited a number of places. Thumba in Kerala, in southern India, was selected as it is near the equatorial region and is ideally suited for ionospheric research in the upper atmosphere, apart from the study of the atmospheric structure. When Dr Sarabhai visited Thumba, the locality had a number of villages and thousands of fishing folk were living in that area. It also had a beautiful ancient church, the St Mary Magdalene Church, and the bishop's house nearby. Dr Sarabhai met many politicians and bureaucrats in order to get the place for building research facilities but it was difficult to obtain permissions. Finally he was asked to see the bishop of Trivandrum, Reverend Father Dr Peter Bernard Pereira. It was a Saturday when Dr Sarabhai met the bishop. The bishop smiled and asked him to meet him the next day, Sunday. That day, after service at the church, the bishop told the congregation, 'My children, I have a famous scientist with me who wants our church and the place I live for the work of space science research. Dear children, science seeks truth by reasoning. In one way, science and spiritualism seek the same divine blessings for doing good. My children, can we give God's abode for a scientific mission?' The church reverberated with a chorus of 'Amen' from the congregation. Subsequently, Reverend Dr Peter Bernard Pereira took the noble decision to dedicate the church building to India's national goal of establishing ISRO. That was where we had our design centre, started rocket assembly, design of filament winding machine and the bishop's house was our scientists' place. The church building has been maintained with love and care ever since and is a reminder to all of us of where the beginnings of our space programme lay. Today it houses the Indian Space Museum. Later, TERLS led to the establishment of the Vikram Sarabhai Space Centre (VSSC) and multiple space centres throughout the country.

When I think of this event, I can see how enlightened spiritual and scientific leaders work harmoniously for larger goals. Later, a new church and new schools were established in record time at Thumba. The birth of TERLS and then VSSC gave India the capability to design, develop and produce world-class rocket systems. India developed the capability of launching geo-synchronous, sun-synchronous and meteorology spacecraft, communication satellites and remote sensing satellites, thereby providing fast communication, weather forecasting and also locating water resources for the country. Dr Vikram Sarabhai is no longer among us, neither is Reverend Dr Peter Bernard Pereira, but I see them as flowers that blossom to bring value to others' lives. This is described in the Bhagwad Gita: 'See the flower, how generously it distributes perfume and honey. It gives to all, gives freely of its love. When its work is done, it falls away quietly. Try to be like the flower, unassuming despite all its qualities.'

This story of how we got a rocket-launching facility is an inspirational message for all generations. It is about the integration of minds. Nowhere in the world has a church been given for scientific research; it has happened only in India. It is a great message to be spread. The message is, the best component of religion can be transformed into a spiritual force that will shape society.

As I continued my work at what became ISRO, I came into contact with Dr Sarabhai more and more often. He was giving shape to his vision of the country's space programme by setting up the facility at Thumba, by conceiving the idea of India building its own SLV and at the same time building a Rocket-Assisted Take-Off System (RATO), which would enable military aircraft to take off even from the most hostile terrain. I would be amazed at the way his mind worked—the clear ideas and the ability to look ahead even when such things were not apparent to the rest of us.

Dr Sarabhai's leadership qualities were such that he could inspire even the junior-most person in an organization with a sense of purpose. In my opinion, there were some basic qualities that made him a great leader. Let me mention them one by one.

Firstly, he was always ready to listen. In Indian institutions, what often hinders growth is the reluctance of those at the top to listen to their juniors and subordinates. There is a belief that all decisions and ideas must come in a top-to-down manner. The line between leadership and bullying is a thin one. Dr Sarabhai amazed us often with the amount of trust he placed in us. At INCOSPAR we were essentially a bunch of young, inexperienced engineers with large quantities of zeal and enthusiasm within us. He harnessed this youthful spirit by giving us a vision and by also making us feel that we were part of a larger whole. His visits to Thumba would be preceded by days of feverish activity, as each of us wanted to show him something new that had been developed—be it a new design, new fabrication or even a new administrative process. He groomed us to become leaders in our own rights.

A second quality that I believe stands a leader in good stead is the ability to think creatively. When Dr Sarabhai decided that we should build the SLV and the RATO, there appeared to be no immediate link between the two. Yet, time and again it was proved to us that his thoughts and tasks that initially seemed random were actually deeply interconnected. I was quick to realize this, and made up my mind early on to remain alert and focused in order to be assigned unusual and demanding tasks to be implemented at my laboratory. In the larger perspective, Dr Sarabhai envisioned India's space programme as an integrated whole, which would encompass the design and manufacture of rockets, satellites, launch vehicles and launch facilities. A wide-ranging programme for development of rocket fuels, propulsion systems, aeronautics and aerospace materials, tracking systems and instruments also gathered pace at the Space Science and Technology Centre and Physical Research Laboratory at Ahmedabad. When Dr Sarabhai gave shape to a vision to develop rockets in India, he was questioned, along with the political leadership, on the relevance of such a programme when a vast majority in the country was battling the demons of hunger and poverty. Yet, he was in agreement with Jawaharlal Nehru that India could only play a meaningful role in the affairs of the world if the country was self-reliant in every manner, and should be able to apply advanced technologies to alleviate real-life problems. Thus our space programme was never simply a desire to be one among an elite group of nations, neither was it a matter of playing catch-up with other countries. Rather, it was an expression of the need for developing indigenous capabilities in telecommunications, meteorology and education.

A third quality that I observed in Dr Sarabhai, and which I have tried to incorporate in my own way of working, was an ability to build teams. Dr Sarabhai had an uncanny knack of spotting the right person for the job. He would then back the person completely even if he or she lacked experience. He also had his own ways of raising morale—a much-required ability in a leader, particularly in a field like ours, where we often had to battle odds and failures. When required he could make the bleakest scenario appear not so dark, he would praise us even if we had not completely reached our goal if he felt that it was justified, and he never stinted on using humour to alleviate the tensions inherent in our field. All of this helped him build teams and institutions that remained steadfastly loyal to him and his vision. Each person knew he could contribute, and that the contribution would be recognized and valued.

And finally, that great quality of his—to look beyond failures. I remember that for one of his visits to Thumba we had prepared a demonstration of the nose-cone jettisoning mechanism of the SLV stage we were working on. The plan was that when Dr Sarabhai pressed a switch, the pyro system would be activated through a timer circuit. But when he pressed the switch as requested, nothing happened. I was in a state of shock, along with my colleague Pramod Kale, who had designed and integrated the timer circuit. We quickly gauged the problem as being one within the timer, and gave direct access to the pyro after detaching it. When Dr Sarabhai pressed the switch this time, the pyros were fired and the nose cone was jettisoned, as it was supposed to. Dr Sarabhai congratulated us on our work, but there was a thoughtful look on his face as he said goodbye. That evening I was asked to meet him at the Kovalam Palace Hotel in Trivandrum.

I had an uneasy feeling as I made my way there. He met me with his usual warmth and spoke about the rocket launching station. Then he turned to the incident of the morning. I readied myself to be upbraided. Instead, Dr Sarabhai delved into deeper issues—were we unenthused by the job, or was it not challenging enough for us? After talking to me, we finally came upon a reason behind that morning's failure. We needed an integrated space for the system integration of all our rocket stages and rocket systems. After pinpointing this reason, Dr Sarabhai stayed up late into the night redefining roles and coming up with a new department—the Rocket Engineering Section.

As I have mentioned, mistakes and failures are a part of every project, particularly in ones like ours where we work on a number of systems and various teams are responsible for different stages, where even a small error at one stage can put to waste years of hard work. Dr Sarabhai used these mistakes as gateways for innovation and the development of new systems. He had the ability to look beyond the specific error and read what lay behind it. He kept room for errors and instead tried to analyze how we could make them manageable, so that we ruled the project, and not our fear of failure.

The place ISRO now has in the community of space-faring nations is second to none. It has developed world-class satellites, satellite and rocket launchers and has provided invaluable service to the country in the fields of scientific research, innovation, education and telecommunication facilities. So much so that it has sent an orbiter to the moon, the Chandrayaan 1, and will soon send a probe to Mars. All of this grew from the seeds planted by Dr Sarabhai and nurtured by the likes of Satish Dhawan and subsequent chairmen of the organization.

My relationship with Vikram Sarabhai was a deeply emotional and intellectual one. Time and again he placed his faith in me to lead teams that would design and develop mechanisms to take India further and further on her course to becoming a self-reliant nation, in terms of science and defence. He took the young rocket engineer sitting before him, answering his questions with honesty and clarity, into his fold and shared his own dream of building rockets and missiles with him. He stood by me in moments of crisis and doubt, of failure and success, guiding me, pointing me on the right path when necessary or showing me where the path lay when I was confused. He was a giant among men, and I was fortunate that I could grow in his shadow.

Dr Sarabhai's death came as a cruel blow to me, not least because it was completely unexpected. In December 1971, I spoke to him from Delhi, updating him about a missile panel meeting that I had just attended there. He was in Thumba then and asked me to meet him at Trivandrum airport after landing from Delhi, as he would be on his way to Bombay. That meeting never happened. I landed at Trivandrum a few hours later to hear the news that Dr Sarabhai had passed away from a cardiac arrest. I came to know that he died an hour after our conversation. The man who nurtured scientists and engineers who would go on to head important scientific projects of the country, who was a great scientist and a leader, was no more there for us to turn to. But before his going he had equipped us with the knowledge, confidence and foresight required to take on all sorts of challenges, and I believe that our greatest homage to him was for each of us to realize our own true potential, which he had spotted at the very first meeting.

It is perhaps a pattern in my life that those closest to me pass away suddenly, without warning. What has that taught me? For each person I lost I found a new layer of grief to cover myself with, and each time I tried to bring something of their essence into my own being—be it unconditional love, kindness and piety. In Dr Sarabhai's case, perhaps it was the ability to look ahead—to plan, to build and to create. If I have achieved even a part of that through my actions and through the various roles I have been entrusted with, I consider myself successful in living up to the expectations of this great visionary of India.

a life in science

After India conducted the second nuclear test at Pokhran in 1998, in whose development I played a part, I was given various epithets. The one that has stayed with me even after so many years and beyond the years of my presidency is Missile Man. It amuses me vastly when I hear myself being called that, for it sounds more the name for a child's action figure than of a man of science that I believe myself to be. Yet, it also carries all the love and respect that has been showered on me by so many in this country. To me it also symbolizes some sort of culmination of my journey into the realm of science, rocketry and engineering. The beginning of this journey stretches a long way back into time—so long that when I think back I wonder if it all happened to me, or is it some story that I myself read in a book somewhere? But of course, all that went into making me a person who chose the path of science really did happen, and remembering it now is like taking a journey upriver—from the delta to the source, further and further upstream I drift, till I reach the point when I was still a boy, trying to find my path in life.

In many ways my real education began after I left Rameswaram for high school at Ramanathapuram. As I have written earlier, it was the first time I stepped out of the protective embrace of Rameswaram, my mother and everything else that was familiar. I was very much a shy small-town boy then, afraid to speak out much. It was at Schwartz High School that I had my first brush with the wonders of science, and had it explained to me in a manner that set my mind alight. At that school there was a teacher called Reverend Iyadurai Solomon. He struck up a relationship of great openness and trust with me. In him, I found the guide that I needed to show me the path forward.

I was fascinated by the flight of birds in the sky. I could watch them for hours, looking at their flight patterns and paths in the skies above me. The desire to fly and be one among them had grown within me from a young age. One day, while studying the physics of flight, Reverend Iyadurai Solomon took a bunch of us students to the seashore. There he pointed out the birds, and standing by the sea, with the roar of the waves in our ears, the harsh cries of cranes and seagulls as they soared around us, he opened up a new world of aerodynamics, aeronautical design and jet-streams and airflows to us. I was one among a group of fifteen year olds, and for me, it was perhaps the most important lesson in science till then. Suddenly, what for me till then had been a matter of fascination, was now explained and made clear. It was as though I had been looking out from behind a cloudy glass window. Now the window had been thrown open and I was looking out into the world with wide-open eyes, thirsting to know more.

As I made my way through school and then into college at St Joseph's, Tiruchirapalli, there were many more such moments lying in wait for me. I had realized early on that I needed to keep my mind and ears open, my brain sharpened and focused and there was nothing that I could not learn or absorb if it came my way. At St Joseph's, when introduced to the concept of subatomic physics by Professor Chinnadurai and Professor Krishnamurthy, I started thinking for the first time about the hidden world of matter and decay that is present all around us. I learnt about half-life periods and the radioactive decay of substances, and suddenly, the world seemed a lot different from the solid certainties that had formed it earlier. I also got thinking about the so-called dualities of science and spirituality. Were they really all that different from each other as they were made out to be? If at a subatomic level particles can become unstable and disintegrate, how far was it removed from the state of all human life? Science sought to provide answers to all natural phenomena, and spirituality helped us understand our place in the entire scheme of the universe. While one looked at it through the solid certainties of mathematics and formulae, spirituality did so by opening up the mind and heart to experiences and by going deeper within one's own self. Hazily, it started getting apparent to me that the connections between what was becoming my world and the one my father inhabited were not that far removed from one another.

From Tiruchirapalli I went to MIT to study aeronautical engineering. Here, the sight of two decommissioned aircraft reignited my desire to know everything about the fascinating world of human flight. I was drawn towards them like a moth to a flame and realized there was no career possible for me that did not take me into the realm of these man-made flying objects. At MIT, three teachers shaped this desire and took it from a wish to the path of reality. They were Professor Sponder, an Austrian who taught me technical aerodynamics, Professor K.A.V. Pandalai, who taught aero-structure design and analysis, and Professor Narasingha Rao, who taught us theoretical aerodynamics.

These three teachers showed me just how fascinating a subject aeronautics is. What we perceive as movement and flow is broken down into components that explain how and why objects move in the air. I lost myself in exploring the complex world of fluid dynamics, modes of motion, shock waves, shock-wave drag and more. At the same time the structural features of aeroplanes became clearer to me, and I studied with infinite gusto all about biplanes, monoplanes, tailless planes and many other such areas of study.

There were many moments that occurred while I was at MIT when I found myself avidly exploring the world of science. All this was happening at a period in the country's history when, starting from the prime minister himself—Jawaharlal Nehru—great emphasis was being laid on the development of the scientific temperament. All around me, especially in an educational institution like ours, I observed that we were being encouraged to leave behind traditional ways of thinking and embrace this new climate. It was best if we used scientific methods in the pursuit of knowledge. Brought up as I was steeped in the religious climate of Rameswaram, I found this very difficult to do. Instead, I found myself giving shape to my earlier glimmerings of the essential oneness of science and spirituality. I could not make myself acknowledge that sensory perceptions were the only source of knowledge and truth. I had been brought up with the lesson that true reality lay beyond the material world, in the spiritual realm, and that true knowledge lay in exploring the inner self. Now, I was becoming more and more a part of another world—where proofs and experiments and formulae held sway. Gradually

I learnt to work out my own stand on this, though it took many years to crystallize.

Finally, I emerged from the portals of MIT a certified engineer, yet I still had to learn a lot about the world of rockets and missiles that were going to be where my career lay in the future. All I knew then was that a great big world lay open for me to explore, and I was determined to do as much of it from high up, way up in the skies.

After some years at the DTD&P (Air) where I was part of various teams that designed and built systems ranging from a vertical landing and take-off platform to what was termed a Hot Cockpit, I found myself at the Aeronautical Development Establishment (ADE) in Bangalore. It was here, I realize now, that I had my first big opportunity at innovation and learning to build something from scratch—this was to become a recurring pattern in my career. At ADE, based on my preliminary studies on ground-handling equipment, it was decided that an indigenous hovercraft prototype should be designed and developed as a Ground Equipment Machine (GEM). The director of ADE, Dr Mediratta, put together a small team of four, and told me to head it.

It was a massive challenge for us. There was neither much literature on it, nor a person who was experienced in this sort of technology whom we could turn to for advice. There were no pre-existing designs or standard components that we could use. In fact, there was nothing much the team had going for it, other than knowing that we had to build a successful flying machine. It was an astounding challenge, I think now, for a group of engineers who had not built a machine ever, leave alone a flying one. We were given three years to complete the project, and we spent the first few months simply floundering, trying to find our feet. Then at one point I decided that we just needed to go ahead with the available hardware and take things as they came. Despite the huge challenge, it was also a project right after my heart and fired my imagination too. We moved from the design process into development after a few months.

By now, I was a much more assertive and confident individual, yet my small-town middle-class roots could never leave my soul. Pushed into a world where one needed to direct the work of others while facing the questions and doubts of senior colleagues, it had the same effect on me as an iron that has been forged in fire. People like me, who are intrinsically shy, with the added quality of coming from a different background than my city-bred colleagues, tend to remain hidden in the shadows unless something or someone pushes us centre stage. I understood that I had got that push and was determined to use all my knowledge and ingenuity to make the hovercraft project a success. There were many within the organization who questioned the relevance of the project—of the amount of time and money it was using up. They questioned my role in it, too. But my team and I just put our heads down and continued to work. Slowly, stage-by-stage, the prototype started to take shape. As had once happened when Professor Srinivasan rejected my design work at MIT and I redid my entire work in the span of two nights, I again found now that the mind is unbelievably elastic. It can expand as much as you let it, and once it opens up, there are no barriers—the belief in yourself that comes as a result is something no one can take away from you.

The project was christened Nandi, and had the blessings of the then defence minister, V.K. Krishna Menon. He firmly believed that this was the beginning of the development of defence equipment in India. He keenly followed our work and after one year, when he inspected the progress we had made, he told Dr Mediratta that Kalam and his team are sure to succeed.

Indeed, we did succeed. Before our three years were up, we produced a fully working prototype and were ready to show it to the minister. Krishna Menon flew in the Nandi and I piloted it—though his security detail would have wished otherwise—and I realized for the first time the sheer joy and exhilaration of creating something, based on our knowledge and teamwork, that was a first for the country. Unfortunately, the story of Nandi does not have a happy ending. Once Krishna Menon was out of office, his successors did not share his optimism about the use of the hovercraft. It became a controversial subject and was finally shelved. If anything could bring me down to earth and show me that sometimes the sky was not the limit, it was this rude lesson—that often there are powers greater than yours who dictate the consequences of your work. My other lesson was that while there are areas that I cannot influence, I can certainly do my work to the best and to the most of my abilities, as finally that is all that remains in one's hands. And who knows just where the consequences of our actions lie? While I was still trying to recover from the disappointment of Nandi not being put to the use for which it was created, a chain of events led Professor M.G.K. Menon of TIFR to come see it and question me about it. This finally ended with me going to work for INCOSPAR as a rocket engineer, under the direction of Dr Vikram Sarabhai.

After I went to work at INCOSPAR and then ISRO, I was entrusted with the development of various types of rockets and space vehicles, ranging from sounding rockets to rocket payloads to satellite launch vehicles. It was Dr Sarabhai's vision to develop India's space programme as one where various developmental work happened concurrently, and I was fortunate to be a part of a number of such projects. However, the one that I regard as my most complex challenge has to be the development of the SLV. I was leading a mammoth project of developing a launch vehicle that would put satellites into orbit. It had the potential to not only enhance our position as a technology-driven nation, it would also generate revenues for us by providing launch facilities to other countries who wished to use the SLV to put their satellites into orbit. I have described in detail my journey in the building of SLV in my book, *Wings of Fire*. It was an extraordinarily difficult journey on account of many factors. There were the invariable complications that arise when a project of this size is developed. We were given a budget—both in terms of time and resource—and it was my responsibility to see that we achieved the result within that budget. It was also a time of great personal stress for me. For within the space of three years I lost three dear ones—Ahmed Jalalluddin, my father and my mother. It was only by drowning myself in my work and keeping my mind firmly focused on the end result that we needed to deliver that I was able to bring the project to fruition.

If I am asked now as to what were the biggest lessons I learnt in the development of the SLV, I will say there are three aspects. There was the first revelation to me about the role of science and technology, research and engineering in the development of a country. In the number of teams that were working on the SLV there were scientists, researchers and engineers. Who did what and where—as a team leader, I was meant to draw lines and give direction. I learnt that science is open-ended and exploratory. That it sets out to find answers like a traveller goes on a voyage. It is, in fact, a voyage into all that is possible and all that will one day be explained and made possible. Science is a joy and passion. Development, on the other hand, is a closed loop. It takes the work done by scientists and moves it a few steps further. It does not allow for mistakes and exploration. In fact, it uses mistakes for making modifications and upgradations. So where the scientists showed us the way and opened up possibilities that enabled us to build an indigenously designed and developed launch vehicle, the engineers kept us on the path of results, given the time and resources we had on hand. For a project of this nature to succeed, it needed all these parts to work in tandem and in sync, like the pieces of an orchestra.

The second lesson that came to me was about the nature of commitment. In those years, while I myself thought of little else other than the project, there were many others like me who put in tremendous amounts of hard work and passion into it. Yet, more valuable words of wisdom on this were never said to me than those by Wernher von Braun. A giant in the field of rocketry, von Braun had developed the V-2 missiles that destroyed London during World War II. Later, he was inducted into NASA's rocketry programme, where he created the Jupiter missile that was the first missile with a high range. He was a scientist, designer, engineer, administrator and a technology manager. He was, indeed, the father of modern rocketry. I had the privilege of flying with him when he visited India, when I received him at Chennai and escorted him to Thumba. His words to me about the whole nature of our work are still ingrained in my mind. 'You should always remember that we don't just build on successes, we also build on failures.' On the inevitable hard work and dedication required by those in our profession he said, 'Hard work is not enough in rocketry. It is not a sport where mere hard work can fetch you honours. Here, not only do you have to have a goal, but you also need strategies to achieve it as fast as possible.

'Total commitment is not just hard work, it is total involvement. It is also about setting a goal. It is having a goal in front of you that makes a difference to the final outcome of your hard work.' And these words, that I believe I did follow: 'Do not make rocketry your profession, your livelihood—make it your religion, your mission.' At that time in life I put everything other than the SLV project on hold. I also learnt to manage stress. It is the way your mind handles the difficulties that are strewn in the path of your goal that determines the result. I truly believe we need these difficulties in order to enjoy the final success of any mission.

And this leads on to my third lesson from the SLV project— the ability to deal with setbacks and learn from them. It is now well known that the first experimental flight trial of the SLV-3 ended in disaster—the vehicle plunged into the sea. Stage 1 performed perfectly. It was at the second stage that things went out of control. The flight was terminated after 317 seconds and the vehicle's remains, including the fourth stage with the payload, splashed into the sea, 560 kilometres off Sriharikota.

I was numbed beyond belief at the turn of events. Yes, I had experienced failures and setbacks earlier, but this, coming at the end of years of back-breaking hard work, was difficult to absorb. I had no answers as the thought kept racing round and round in my head—'What went wrong?' I was at the end of my physical capabilities as I had been putting up with enormous stress and now, when all of it had come to nought, there was nothing I could say to myself or to those around me that made any sense. Finally, all I could think of was sleep. I had to sleep, I told myself, before I could go any further on this path of analysis. I remember I must have slept for many hours, and was awoken gently by Dr Brahm Prakash. He was then my boss, but at the time he came to me only as an elder, with concern. He woke me up and made me accompany him to the mess for a meal. We ate together and all the time he gave me solace by not uttering a single word about the launch. The analysis and the rebuilding of the mission would come later. At that moment in time we were just two men, tired beyond belief, yet knowing that what we had created would not come to waste. We knew we had more mountains to climb and higher peaks to conquer in the days to come, but right then he took me under his wings and did what a parent would do to a child after he has lost that coveted race—give him food, let him rest and let him think where the next step lies.

And that was perhaps the most important lesson I learnt from SLV-3. That humaneness, generosity and understanding can never let you down. At the end of the day, when goals have been set and mapped, when the path has been traversed and obstacles met head on, it is only the values of humanity that will bring true succour. To be able to be gentle and forgiving, compassionate and kind are finally all we need to be in times to come, whether we develop missiles or teach in a school; whether we hold high offices or are parents bringing up children in this confusing world of ours.

My journey into the world of science goes on much further from here—from ISRO I moved to DRDO, where I was part of the teams that built India's first indigenous missile systems—the Prithvi, Trishul, Nag and Agni. How they were built and the paths they led us on I have chronicled earlier too. While working on them, not only did I understand and assimilate the knowledge about new areas of science and rocketry, I also learnt to innovate, to lead more effectively, to communicate and to absorb both setbacks and successes.

Why do I need to tell these stories? Perhaps because I feel that in the diverse range of subjects and people I have dealt with, I have encountered almost every aspect of life that can be bewildering. I worked my way through them, and if in my recounting I can help others in similar situations understand the vagaries of life, then I will believe that this journey of mine has been lived not just for me but for countless others too.

I am a well in this great land
Looking at its millions of boys and girls
To draw from me
The inexhaustible divinity
And spread His grace everywhere
As does the water drawn from a well.

miles to go

This clutch of stories consists of little vignettes of my life that touch upon moments and people, time and places that have left a deep impact upon me. Needless to say, when one begins to remember and recount such moments from one's life—and if it has been as full and busy as mine—there are hundreds more that can be told. In my mind, my years as the scientific adviser to the Government of India when India conducted its second nuclear test, my retirement and dedication to teaching thereafter and my years as the President of India, all hold stories of innumerable challenges and learning.

As I stepped further and further into the glare of the media with the launch of Agni and subsequent events, I had to draw from the lessons I learnt early in life to deal with all sorts of decisions and conundrums. My priorities and aims also underwent subtle changes. Whereas earlier I was involved more with implementing and doing, now I entered a more reflective period when I spent time thinking, writing and talking with people from all walks of life. As the years went by, I found that my great interest now lay in interacting more and more with the youth of the country. I went on to write a number of books which were successful, perhaps because the readers recognized them to be mission statements of a man who saw a certain vision of India for the year 2020, and who was trying to work on the vision and articulate it to the country at the same time. My work on my books, *India 2020, Wings of Fire, Ignited Minds* and others have been deeply satisfying for the great enthusiasm with which they were received by the reading public of the country.

While I expressed my vision and dream for the country through my lectures, interactions, articles and books, I also became interested in many other areas of technology. I had the unique experience in the 1990s of helping to formulate the India Vision 2020 strategies. I was given the task of chairing the Technology Information, Forecasting and Assessment Council (TIFAC). In the first meeting of the council itself we took a decision that TIFAC must evolve a plan on how India can be transformed into an economically developed nation by the year 2020. At a time when the economy was growing at around 5 to 6 per cent per annum in GDP, we had to envisage a growth rate of at least 10 per cent per annum consistently for over ten years if the development vision of a billion people was to be fulfilled. This task really ignited the minds of all of us in the council. We debated and arrived at seventeen task teams with over 500 members, who had consultations with over 5,000 people in various sectors of the economy. Committees worked for over two years, resulting in twenty-five reports that we presented to the then prime minister of India on 2 August 1996. This is an excellent example of how different departments and organizations worked in an integrated way for national development. While our work at TIFAC was progressing, I also studied what was being done in the fields of agriculture and information technology with a lot of interest, and that became an abiding passion for me. As I travelled all over the country meeting students and teachers, administrators and officials, I understood that working on a vision was only the first part of my work. Only when one can express the mission, explain it and debate about it does the vision acquire life. I decided to do just that by talking to people wherever I went, about the need to make India a knowledge-based society, a country where technology brings empowerment, yet at the same time we continue to acknowledge and develop our spiritual dimensions.

My term as the President of India, from 2002 to 2007, I now look back on as one long lesson in understanding the wonder that is India. The media gave me the name People's President, which was picked up by many across the country.

And I must say I was happy to be referred to as such. When I started my tenure, I was very sure that I intended to spend as much time as possible touring this endlessly complex and fascinating country that is ours. I wanted to see how people lived in different parts, the environment that formed their lives, what their problems are and how these were being solved—or were they being solved at all. It was said that as President of the country, I toured it more than perhaps any other before me. From the slopes of Siachen to the beautiful northeastern states, from the far western regions of the country to the deep south, I went almost everywhere except Lakshwadeep (which will remain a regret). I travelled by road, by air and even by rail on three occasions, when the old presidential railway carriage was refurbished and upgraded with modern facilities like satellite mapping, and I have to say I saw the country from all kinds of angles, for which I will be eternally grateful.

What did I learn from the hundreds, no, millions of men, women and children that I met in these years? I learnt that as a society we are trained to not question the status quo. It requires a lot of coaxing and encouragement to make even the young people I met in schools to open up and ask their questions. At the same time, this does not mean that the questions are not there. They are waiting, bubbling at the surface. Once the gates are opened, the dams burst forth with eagerness and inquisitiveness. I have been asked questions on science, technology, space, the arts and I have been asked questions on why I have remained a bachelor and why I wear my hair the way I do! To each question I tried to give an answer—one that was well thought out, sincere and as detailed as possible. I also told them that I myself am still very much a seeker. I came to them as much to speak and debate as to seek the answers that I was looking for myself. I understood then what it means to be an Indian, what it means to be a man or a woman in this country, how each one of us shapes the society while we each live our lives, and what can one do with this understanding.

The years of my presidency also had its share of political upheavals, which I have written about in my last book, *Turning Points*. As the constitutional head of the country, I became intricately involved in the democratic process. The way Parliament and other institutions functioned, and how the President can bring about changes in the areas of his influence were thoughts that preoccupied a lot of my time.

After my term as President was over, I happily returned to my earlier life of teaching and lecturing that took me all over the country and abroad. If possible, I was perhaps as busy, if not more, as I worked tirelessly to push my favourite projects, India

2020 and Providing Urban Amenities in Rural Areas (PURA). I have continued to meet students, pursued research in universities in India and abroad, and contributed my views on national issues. I visit remote areas in order to talk to students there and give them a larger vision for their future. They often question me on many things—from what subjects they should study in the higher classes to infrastructural issues in their towns and districts.

This book, however, is not meant to be a linear account of my life. I have done that earlier. This little book is like a resting place on a long and winding road. It is that spot you spy on the highway where you veer away from the onrushing traffic to stop and watch the rest of the world pass by while you mull over the journey you have taken so far. It is perhaps a little stop on the train that I took from Madras to Dehra Dun once upon a time, when I saw the country from the southern tip to the northern reaches for the first time. This time, however, my eyes are not focused on the destination alone. I can turn back and wonder at the magical beginning of life—I can see my father walking home with his coconuts, his mind alight with prayer; I can follow the movements of my mother's hands as she prepares the chutneys and sambar and rice for the day for us and as she beckons me to come sit by her on the kitchen floor; I can close my eyes and hear the roar of waves and the crashing of the wind against the trees as the cyclones strike Rameswaram; I can still feel the tiredness in my legs and arms after a day that began and ended with delivering newspapers and then collecting the money for them. I can also hear voices and words as clearly as though they were spoken yesterday. I can hear my father tell me, 'I know you have to go away to grow. Does the seagull not fly across the sun, alone and without a nest? You must forego your longing for the land of your memories to move into the dwelling place of your greater desires; our love will not bind you, nor will our needs hold you.'

At this restful spot I can stop and wait for my co-travellers to walk by me one more time. From Pakshi Lakshmana Sastrygal, Reverend Iyadurai Solomon, Ahmed Jalalluddin to Dr Vikram Sarabhai, Professor Satish Dhawan and Dr Brahm Prakash, I think of many others like them who deeply influenced me, moulded and shaped my thoughts and intellect. While telling their stories, their presence has become more deeply felt than ever before for me. The germination of thoughts planted in my soul by these people has continued years after they left my side. When I have shared these with you, my reader, I hope some seeds have been planted in your minds too, the way they once came to me. This transfer of thoughts and ideas, ideals and principles is a part of the circle that is life.

Hard work and piety, study and learning, compassion and forgiveness—these have been the cornerstones of my life. I have now shared with the world the roots of these features. In fact, any life that has been lived to the full, when talked about with others, is a treasure house of thoughts and feelings that add lustre to the wonder that is life. In the process, if they also give my readers wings and help them to fire their dreams, I believe I would have played my small part in the scheme of life that destiny placed me in.

acknowledgements

My Journey is indeed an account of a life full of events. For nearly twenty-two years, my friend, Harry Sheridon, has been with me and become part of many events as they unfolded. With me, he has seen many happy times as well as those filled with problems. Through thick and thin, Sheridon has always been with me and has been of great assistance in whatever I do. May God bless him and his family. I would like to thank Sudeshna Shome Ghosh of Rupa Publications, who was with me from conception, design to the shaping of the book. She has been following up continuously, with perseverance, in bringing it out. I greet her for her efforts.